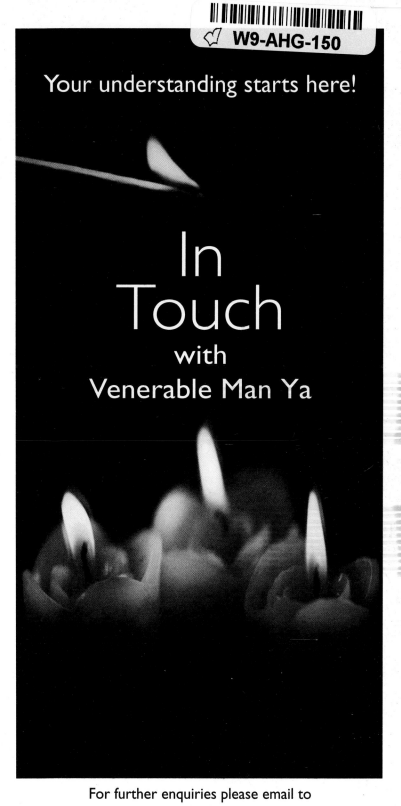

Your understanding starts here!

In Touch
with
Venerable Man Ya

For further enquiries please email to

shihmanya@maxis.net.my

WELLNESS

In
Touch
with
Venerable Man Ya

by Bronwen Eckstein

Foreword
Venerable Man Ya

Religious philosophy should be understood with simple words and applicable in daily life. This means that we should not find it difficult to understand what religious teaching or philosophy is trying to say.

However, many people find it difficult to understand the philosophy of living a mindful life – that concerns me a lot! When Buddha realized the truth, he taught us how to live a life of freedom but because of our deluded mind we ended up not understanding his message. For instance, we have the mistaken idea that life is suffering and so we must leave our everyday world to seek liberation. This resulted in religious practice being separated from mundane or ordinary living. Because of this misunderstanding of Buddhism, people thought they had to leave their routines in order to practice. So people give all sorts of excuses for not practicing: "I need to find the time to practice", "I need to go away to practice", and "I can't practice because I don't have the time and can't go away."

So we delay our practice, brood over the past, and think about the future – except to live in the moment. We fail to realize that the teaching helps us to enjoy the present moment if we are mindful in our actions. Instead, we prefer to live in the past and worry about the future. However, the teaching can be useful in our daily routine. So we need to emphasize that it's not tomorrow, it's not the next life, and it's not the supramundane or esoteric life that we are talking about where we can apply the Buddha's teaching. It's right here in our life at this place, time, and moment.

Religious teaching should not make people arrogant or exclusive, in the mistaken idea that mindfulness and wisdom is only for certain groups of people. Let us use the teaching in our families, in schools, in hospitals, in businesses and in the everyday world where we live. Let's use it now, and not put it off to some other time hoping to be closer to peace and happiness when we can have it right here in the present moment.

Man Ya

Venerable Man Ya Shih

Venerable Man Ya

More about Venerable Man Ya

The Nan Hua Temple in Bronkhorstspruit, South Africa, rises like a displaced pagoda in the middle of fields of sun-bleached highveld grass. For the Abbess of this Buddhist temple, these contrasts and contradictions were opportunities to fire up the great melting pot of modern culture. Venerable Man Ya (47), who joined the temple in May 2001, was the first female Abbess to serve as *Director* of the temple and Buddhist centre. The Fo Guang Shan (Buddha's Light Mountain) Order was established in South Africa eleven years ago. As *Director* Man Ya oversaw temple projects as well as the development of the new multimillion-rand temple. Now she is dedicating her life as a travelling monastic to help as many as possible to heal their relationships, bodies and minds.

"We want people to be able to have wisdom, light and creativity in their work," says Man Ya. The diminutive nun, who takes just one main meal a day, chose monastic life in the mid-Eighties after scaling the corporate ladder in her native Taiwan, and completing a degree in Information Systems In Texas, USA. She has travelled widely. After taking her vows in 1988, she worked in the USA and South America, venturing into countries such as Paraguay and Argentina, before moving to Malaysia, where she published her first book on the practice of Buddhism. She has also travelled to many African countries, and to India.

Venerable Man Ya's principle aim is to demystify Buddhism and reveal a fresh, Western relevance for this ancient Eastern wisdom. "People have become mis-educated and they have become attached to the rituals or to the words. I think that if the Buddha was around today he would do things differently. We have to become skilful in our approach to working with people," she says. "We are not trying to reach everyone. People have different pasts and different needs. I say to Buddhists that where there isn't a temple they should take their children to church. Children need to learn about morality somewhere. They need to learn to love themselves. The religion doesn't matter, what matters is that we help people to open their minds and to awaken. Buddhism is here for all people to come and see if this is what they want." She maintains that religion is not nation-specific. The growth of Buddhism on the African continent is part of global efforts to develop humanistic

Buddhism under the Fo Guang Shan Order. This worldwide order was started by Venerable Master Hsing Yun, a Chinese monk who moved to Taiwan in 1949 and set about revitalising the Mahayana tradition of Buddhism.

"There is a growing curiosity about Buddhism ... Buddhism is about searching from within to remove the cause of suffering. It's about taking personal responsibility and living one moment at a time," Man Ya says.

Introduction

No man is an island. This applies to women and children too. We are none of us alone and isolated. Even the hermit in his mountain cave is in relationship with the living creatures around him - the trees, the birds and mountain creatures, the earth and the sky. The fact that we are in touch with others, other people,  other creatures, other things, can bring us pleasure or pain. Many people realise that their relationships are the source of great suffering to them. Many people are searching for answers to how to live a more peaceful, more rewarding life. Part of that answer lies in understanding the nature of relationships, and how to bring them into greater harmony.

This book came to being through the energies of Venerable Man Ya, the Abbess of the Nan Hua Temple at Bronkhorstpruit in South Africa. A woman of great vision and deep wisdom, she has dedicated her life to helping people understand the truth about relationships, and to building a greater understanding of Buddhism in the Western world. The book came about through a series of meetings between the Abbess and myself, and contains her answers to my many questions about relationships and life. She tackles a wide range of different relationships – our relationship to our first family, who provide role models for our behaviour the rest of our life, our relationship with our friends, relationships at work, falling in love and the relationship with our life partner and how it changes over the long term. Then there are the relationships we have with other individuals and groups who we do not know – the strangers who move in and out of our lives. We have a relationship with what we consume, whether it is food, drugs, intoxicants, poisons, words, pictures, or concepts. We also have a relationship with the living world, plants, animals and our planet, and beyond all of these, a relationship with our spiritual side and with God or the infinite. In each of these relationships, we can discover ourselves by gently observing our responses, our past reactions and our preconceived ideas, and through introspection we can learn to live a more fulfilled life.

This book is based on Buddhist concepts, which can enrich your own life whatever your religious beliefs. You do not have to believe in Buddhism to put into practice this simple and workable approach. The main purpose of the book is to introduce you to a different view of relationships that could bring you a deeper understanding of others, yourself and the universe. At the end of the book there is a very short guide to basic concepts and practices that can help you deal with difficulties in relationships. Think about these ideas, try them out, and accept or reject them on the basis of their workability.

My humble thanks to Venerable Man Ya for sharing her wisdom and her deep understanding of Buddhism, and for allowing me to write it down.

Bronwen Eckstein
Johannesburg 2003

Contents

Your First Family

Your first family

We live in relationship with others. As a result, all of us have developed ways of dealing with other people. Nevertheless, it is hard to meet a person who does not wish for calmer, happier, deeper, more relaxed, less stressful relationships. Who can claim to be completely in tune with everyone, everywhere? Not many of us.

This book contains some thoughts about relationships and how they can be improved. Because we all learn about relationships by example, from our role models, where do we develop our relationship skills? Most of them are acquired in our first family. Everyone has a first family this lifetime. As a human being you can't survive without adults to take care of you and bring you up. Your first family is the family you're born into. The best school for you is your first family. If you don't have a good environment to start with, you will suffer later. The first three years affect the next eighty.

As a baby, you start life in your mother's womb. For the first ten lunar months, before you are even born, your mom's mood and her family situation affect you as a foetus. Then, the next two years (the first two years of life as a separate person), you are still very vulnerable. Parents are often not geared to the needs of the developing baby. Many parents are still children themselves. They are not yet ready for their own children. They are enjoying sex, but sex is not children. Marriage is not children. They rush into rearing children but they are not yet ready for this awesome responsibility. We have parents who are having babies and are still learning to become mature adults. The children become lost because they have no role models to look up to. Their own parents are still guessing about the best way to bring up children! So they have imperfect role models and make the same mistakes their parents did when they have their own children.

Some babies may have been given up for adoption, or have been left at hospitals or orphanages. Some babies may be brought up in child-headed families. Regardless of the many ways babies are cared for, all young humans are affected by the kind of care they get in the first years of their lives.

Many new parents are afraid to be themselves. They pretend to be knowledgeable. They hide their emotions. They want to do well, they want to be recognised as valuable people, they want to be admired and they want the same thing from their children as they want from the rest of the world. Young children are very scared by these expectations.

How do young children learn? They learn by copying. Children copy their parents' behaviour, their brothers', sisters' and cousins' behaviour, without being aware of it. They think that when they go to school they must do the same as all the other children. So they pick up the patterns that they see around them and they learn from everyone and everything they are in contact with, without being conscious of doing so.

How do you prepare yourself as the first family?

Nobody needs to have a baby. But having a baby does help us to learn more about relationships. Having a baby helps us to learn to be aware and attentive. But being a good worker or business person is not the same as being a good parent. So you need to examine your parenting skills as well as your work skills, if you are both a worker and the parent of a young child.

As a new parent, you need to prepare yourself to give. The child depends on her parents, brothers and sisters, and the relationships she observes help her to learn major lessons about life. So as a parent you need to realise you are the most important role model for your baby as he or she progresses through childhood.

For single children it's important that they be given precious opportunities, from an early age, to learn to be sensitive to the needs of others. If not, others will gradually start to complain about their coldness and laziness as they grow up. So learning how to care for pets, doing chores for their parents or doing something for themselves are all important practices.

As a growing child, what do you need to learn? Having brothers and sisters, you learn to share. You share a home, clothing and food. You share learning. You share rooms and toys. You share the bathroom. You share your parents' love. This learning to share, through caring relationships, then moves to the school, and you learn to share with other pupils and teachers. At school you learn to share a classroom, books, facilities, knowledge.

For each child, the first three years are going to define the next eighty. After that nearly one year in utero, where the baby shares its mother's food, emotions, joy and suffering, the baby is born. The next two years are the most precious. At this time the parents, brothers and sisters can motivate a child to be himself. If a person does not build this feeling of 'real self', does not become emotionally balanced, he or she will never learn to connect with others and build those relationships that are the key to a fulfilled life.

We have to start from the centre first. As a young child, you are the centre of your universe, and you need support to grow strong. How can you give if you're not strong? You need to learn to be strong and balanced first, and this is the most important lesson you learn from your first family. You learn to be accepted for who you are by your first family. You learn to be honest with yourself. Sadly, if you have to pretend to please people in your early years, it will be extremely difficult for you to develop enough strength to build authentic relationships with people later on.

Acceptance of the baby and her true nature are the keys to helping that baby become a fulfilled human being this lifetime. Everyone has a long, long history, going back further than we imagine. The baby brings that with her. She cannot change overnight. As the first family of that baby, you first have to accept her as she is, to help her become strong enough to develop herself further as she grows up.

From the time of conception, until the child is two years old, roughly the first three years of the child's existence, that child needs *recognition, support, care and love*.

When the first family fails ...

What happens if the baby doesn't get these things? He will have another 80 years to feel confused, because he is left raw and sensitive. He will take those first unhappy experiences and bury them in his mind. We don't know what young children absorb. If they get the wrong messages, how can we change them? Babies pick up all sorts of things. They are like sponges, absorbing information and experiences every moment. We think the baby's sleeping, he can't hear. But he picks up everything. Everything is absorbed. We don't know that the problem already exists but the baby has heard or seen confusing, upsetting things, and is puzzled, hurt or even harmed. So we need to be aware that this little being is absorbing everything around him, taking it all in, creating himself with the material we provide.

The baby also starts building relationships with other people. It is not just for us as parents to give our time and attention to this young person, the baby gets involved with the rest of the family and all the other people around him. Now is the time for parents to encourage the baby himself to give. The baby will want to help, to share and to join in.

Let him help! Let him help clean the room, share his toys, share his food and tidy up. Young children may be very messy; they may make mistakes, break things or act in silly ways. A loving family lets the child make mistakes and accepts him as he is while he learns to help. But if the family doesn't let the young child build the habit of helping, of contributing in his early life, it becomes very difficult to develop later.

Giving is balancing – giving brings us into balance. When you are giving, you connect with the greater self. You are not separate any more. You realise great joy. We realise that joy by giving. At the moment we give, we connect with others, we become one. We are no longer alone, no longer lonely. Learning about balancing the self all the time is a lesson that needs to start early. So we need to share that understanding with our little children, and encourage them to build the habit of generosity.

Sadly, nowadays, people are very busy. They are rushed and pressurised. They emphasise efficiency. "Do it right away. No mistakes." If there are no mistakes, there are no chances for learning. So realise the little child will mess up. Parents become exhausted with the pressures of life today. They feel their children are a burden, because as parents they have to do it all themselves. But parents don't realise they deprive children of an opportunity to become one with others, by letting them do things for others. Let your children do things for you; let them help their brothers and sisters. Let them contribute in any way, and let them start as early as they can.

Children are often scared. They try to give, they try to help, but they are shouted at, blamed, ignored or smacked. Their attempts to give through smiling and responding and learning and copying and trying to help are discouraged by parents and family. That makes them insecure. It makes them withdraw into themselves, and it makes them greedy, because there is this emptiness, this hollow inside. They don't appreciate whatever is given thereafter, because they feel incomplete. This apparent greed, this lack of appreciation, starts family feuds. Families break down, with family members fighting against each other. Brothers and sisters learn to hate instead of loving and appreciating each other.

With this kind of emotion at home, the child is going to invite hurt and anger at school, because all the hurt and anger is buried in her mind. It is there, hidden, but ready to show itself. So there is more anger and hurt at school. The disaster of life continues, first in one part of life, then another part. It's a cycle of suffering that never ends.

If you are not yourself, you cannot be a good child. You cannot be a good student. You cannot be a good staff member in an office. If you are able to be yourself at home, in your first family, there's no reason for you to feel lost at school. A good first family will bring continuous balance for the rest of your life.

Like and dislike

If you spend time observing yourself, you will begin to see certain patterns in your behaviour. You like this person. You dislike that one. Whenever you feel strong feelings of like or dislike towards others, you are only cheating yourself thinking there was nothing wrong in your first family. If you think the problem is at the office, it's not. It dates back to your first role models in childhood, in your first family. If you are not balanced in yourself, people are not friendly. There's no escape from that lack of being able to be yourself, and the suffering it causes you inside. This learning to be balanced, learning that it's safe to be *you*, is nurtured in the first family.

What happens when a young child suffers in her first few years of life? The suffering child carries that pain inside, and looks for comfort and support. As she grows up, she starts to think that degrees, money, fame, clothes, cars, houses, relationships are the answer to this lack of happiness. But after she has it all, she still feels lost, because she doesn't realise that the source of her happiness is within – it's the connection to herself - and through that to others - which she never had. This idea of being connected to others is sometimes called 'interbeing' or 'non-self'.

Non-self, non-fear

Why do you have to save money? Is it because you feel scared or insecure? Why do you have to emphasise self, self, self? It's because you're hurt and ignored. Many people, when they hear the words, 'non-self' are terrified. This concept of non-self is scary, because our whole life seems to be centred on preserving ourselves and our individuality. We feel we have to look after ourselves, because no-one else will. There is another view. Letting go of the strict division between ourselves and others allows us to become more rather than less. I become one with others, and in doing so, I find I am not so alone. Non-self is not a painful thing to fear. It is where we begin to see that we are part of a larger existence, part of others, part of nature. We start to 'inter-be'.

In becoming aware that we are not alone, isolated and lonely, we start to see the truth of existence. Our minds become clearer and our hearts become calmer. Non-self simply means a rich and balanced mind. It means your mind is clear and you are living life one moment at a time. You are here, you are aware, you are wakeful. Nothing is wanted, nothing is lacking, nothing is looked for. If you feel there is a lack in your life, it's the ego, which lets you feel hurt, harmed, disadvantaged or irritated. The ego is merely any thought, any concept which takes your awareness away from the moment as it is. Non-self is simply being connected with all beings, with the greater self. It's the wholesome, fulfilled life, it's the ultimate goal we are all seeking, whether we admit it or not.

So the family is helping us to let go of this ego and self. It's the first family that motivates the child to be sensitive to other people's needs, to the parents' needs, to the brother's and sister's needs, to the needs of the dog and the cat. The child learns to find out what others need. What do the pets need? What do the trees need? What do the flowers need? What does the room need? What does the toilet need? And the family members help the child to gradually realise this state of 'no individual'. Look at the word individual – break it down. 'In', 'divided', 'dual'. Individual means separated. We don't need that. If you're divided and separated, you feel alone and scared.

It's not a burden for parents to raise a child. It's a blessing, because you are helping another being realise unity. You don't have to make *things* right. *Things* are not important. You have to *make the mind balanced*. That is your role as a parent.

Making the mind balanced

What is a balanced mind? To have a balanced mind means to live our life one moment at a time. When our mind is balanced, we are not easily upset or angered, or pulled foolishly in different directions by our cravings and desires. How can you be aware and mindful of this moment? You have to connect with the people, the environment, at that point in time. So you help your child start to practice this 'being mindful'. Start early. Start helping your child to feel what it is like in other people's shoes. Help him practice mindfulness[1] with you, his parents, his sisters, his brothers, his pets, and his friends. Living our life one moment at a time means being actively involved and giving your full attention and concentration to what you are doing now, this instant. So that's the purpose of the first family. After children grow up, they will share what you have taught them. They will help other human beings to do the same thing – and by helping others, they also improve themselves by concentrating on

---

[1] *Mindfulness is a key element of Buddhist practice. See chapter ten.*

what children need, and who they are. This is a skilful way of being a parent.

What do we mean by skilful?

Let's talk more about being skilful[2]. In order to act with skill (sometimes called 'skilful means'), you must be aware and enlightened about what is going on. You need to understand reality, realising and knowing what is needed, so you can act in the right way at the right time for the best result. If I ask, "What's wrong with you? Why don't you have any appetite?" and then make my own assumptions, that means I don't really understand enough about you. I don't have skilful means. I am just guessing, 'It's this' or 'It's that'. My judgement and knowledge are lacking. If you need vegetables, and I give you a banana, that's not skilful means. If you are lacking banana, and I offer you an apple, that's not skilful means. I give you bread but you need an orange, giving bread is not skilful means. If I offer you a training course, and what you want is marriage and children, my offering would not be skilful. If I want you to marry me, but you want to study further, my wedding proposal would also not be skilful, because it would be done without my taking the trouble to understand your deepest wishes, and respect them, and help you meet them.

The trouble is, people develop 'skilful means' only as they become enlightened. To develop skilful means, we have to check ourselves. Are we kind enough? Are we too arrogant? Are we just assuming what others need, instead of really listening to them and observing them closely and kindly? Are we letting people tell us and then just going ahead and doing something else? Or are we modifying our own views, to better serve the other person? If we think we know the answers and reject other people's thoughts, we have to stop and examine ourselves. Am I arrogant? Am I ignorant? With this openness, you will realise how wrong you were. Then skilful means will be available to you.

Children also teach us to be more skilful, because they are helping us to be better parents, helping us to practice mindfulness. Every being is so different, every day they are new. People are different every day so you also have to be aware of who they are *today* and what they need *today* for you to be there for them. And that is skilful means. There's not only one way to relate to a person over many years. That is not skilful, because people change, the circumstances change. So parents have all sorts of opportunities to

---

[2] *Buddhists do not blame or punish. When we behave in ways that do not help ourselves or others, this is considered to be lacking in skill rather than being harmful or hurtful. We are all learning to be more skilful, and as we do so, we create less harm and suffering to others and to ourselves.*

develop skilful means, and to learn to balance their minds. Many parents have a work environment and colleagues who are also serving as teachers for them. Work colleagues can also help us to be better parents and develop more mindfulness.

What can I do to be a better mother or father?

You can develop heart-to-heart communication with your child. Don't think just because we are a child's parents that we are elders, seniors, that we are wiser and more intelligent. Don't think we are exhausted and have contributed enough already. As parents and children we need each other and we are able to help each other. We learn from each other. We learn from our children just as they learn from us.

What about the mistakes we have made in the past as a mother or father? Never look back. Things that have happened, have happened. They can never be corrected. But that doesn't matter, because we live in the present. Be aware of what you can do now. Be humble. Be selfless. Be honest. Listen deeply to your child. Then you will not cause problems now. The focus is on the now.

Humility is strength, not weakness

Being humble is not a negative quality, as some people seem to think. Only people who are balanced can be humble. Humility comes from a focused mind. Only humility can help us be mindful about what is happening in our lives right now. Being humble gives us strength, so we can see reality clearly. Putting our whole-hearted energy into what we are doing creates a focussed mind.

Humility is not the same as openness. Openness is the result, but humility is the cause. If you don't try to let go and be humble, you will not reach open-mindedness. So how do you develop humility? You do it by *being with someone you love, trust and respect.* Only then do you feel safe enough to try and let go of your ego. Without this support it is very difficult to develop humility. You look down on others, and think that you are right. You need to cultivate a relationship with someone who truly loves and cares for you. Only when you trust each other, can you take the risk and do the hard work to develop humility. That oneness with a loved one can continually motivate you. So in order to develop humility, you need to develop a relationship in which you are able to give, and where you realise you are loved. That will motivate you for a long time, and the virtue of humility will grow and be strengthened. This is how you and your child can learn and grow together.

People who are not humble have many attachments. They are attached to things, to emotions, to attitudes, to material possessions, to outcomes. These attachments create darkness in the mind. They cloud your perceptions, so you cannot see clearly. Only that whole-hearted attention will allow you to include everything in your awareness. Being humble allows you to see everything, not ignore anything, so you see the whole of reality. As soon as you lose humility, you no longer see the whole. Arrogance brings darkness to your heart that makes you lose the reality, and make mistakes. So if you bring humility into your relationship with your child, you can see clearly what your child needs, and how to behave in the present to be helpful rather than harmful.

In building this new relationship with your child, admit whatever you're feeling. Let it out. Express it. Don't let it stay there, sitting in your heart, unexpressed. Don't regret you did this and did that. That just invites the past to come in to the present, and the past cannot be changed. Humility is like cleansing the mind – letting go of the attachments. Then you can include your child in your heart again. You can feel what they feel, and that is comforting for your child. There will be no rejection from your child if you do that.

Sometimes to become humble is a very difficult thing. We have such strong egos that apologising is difficult. But not apologising creates a distance between you and your child. No matter how hard you try to fix the problem, you can't, because there is such a distance between you. Problems disappear if you are one with others. If you're distant from others, and try to solve the problem, rather than the relationship, there's an even worse problem.

If you can't let go of the issues, you need to admit to yourself that the suffering you are feeling about your child is not really caused by that child. The suffering you feel is not caused by others. Don't look for answers from outside. Admit the problem is within. The problem is not being able to let go. When you realise this, you can stop accusing others. Maybe at first you will not find peace, but at least you won't cause any more problems by accusing others and by being disappointed again and again.

The first step is to look within. Stop complaining and blaming others for causing your suffering. At least, if nothing else, you will know that things happen because of your own actions, and it's not other people's fault. Knowing this allows you to start to take charge of your own life.

This philosophy only works for people who want to be responsible for their fate. It only happens for people who are strong. You need to be strong-willed, responsible and active. If you don't have this kind of character, you won't build self-discipline, self-reliance or freedom.

What hope is there for people who depend so addictively on others? Looking for comfort they will suffer in an endless loop. The Buddhist philosophy is not for everyone. It's only for those clear-minded people who are searching for wisdom within.

Being a working parent

Many parents leave their babies and children in the care of others, and go out to work. It is happening all round us, and there is constant pressure for women to have careers as well as bring up children. What is a skilful way to respond to this?

First of all, what is our work? Why do we work? We work to grow more mature, to become more sensitive to the impermanence of the environment. In the work place you can develop this. But also at work, your heart can become hard, cold and insensitive. What is the purpose of your work? Don't lose the understanding of why you are working. Your children didn't order you to get a big house, a big car or fancy holidays. Oh, no. The children need a caring, supportive family. So there must be other reasons you are working. People enter into a relationship with their work. You become an engineer, a farmer, a musician. The perfect reason for working is to develop sensitivity to the impermanence of life in a way that has meaning for you. That is the ideal reason to develop a career – to help you in your personal growth, which means the development of your character and mind. In work, we connect with people. It need not be complicated.

What about day care?

To send a child out to different people at a very early age is risky. It can do a great deal of damage to the child. Different people are not consistent in their behaviour. Your child gets confused, with one nanny behaving one way, the next behaving differently, one teacher at the day care centre treating your child one way, another treating him differently. At a day care centre, there are children from all sorts of backgrounds, from different families to yours. They are not your child's brothers and sisters. They may not care about him. They may teach him things that are a concern for you. Your child is exposed to people who don't care. Children are picking up patterns of behaviour because they cannot distinguish, they cannot judge. They are so confused, they copy whatever they see; they follow these examples and are punished as a result.

Stay at home if you have a little child. You need to have time for your newborn. You become a missionary if you have a child. What do I mean by 'becoming a missionary?' A missionary is someone who works to advance some cause or idea. Your mission is to bring up your child in the best way you know how. That is your cause, your purpose. You have a plan to help the child grow, using your own perspectives and beliefs. You think about how you are going to love and care for this child. You must be responsible. It's not about money and time, it's about your wisdom to be with and to nurture this new, sensitive little being. This child will also help you change your concepts and purify yourself, because the child is under your roof and will help you on the journey of cultivating purity in yourself. You are actually missionaries for each other.

Learning to be better parents – developing a clear state of mind

How do we learn to be better parents? First, you are not your parents. You can choose to copy their ways of raising children, or change those ways. Some beings have a clearer state of mind. What do we mean by a *clear* state of mind? If you have a clear mind, you are totally aware - your mind is fully in this moment. It rises and dies every moment. It is right here, right now, and is nothing more or less than clear awareness. A clear mind knows without thinking, it has knowledge without effort or emotions. It is pure wisdom. There's no self, no ego, no 'me' at all. You are no longer separate from what happens around you. You never think, 'What's happening?' because you know. And it's no effort. It's not that you have to find out, or think, or reason. The wisdom is just there.

We have an inheritance from our ancestors, but we have our own state of mind. We are all different, at different levels of soul development. You know that if you have four children, they are all different. If you try to teach them all in one way, they will respond differently. In this world, we all have many teachers. Our home environment motivates us to develop our awareness. So does the school, so does the work place. All things are motivators to help us wake up. The end is to be enlightened[3], to wake up. Some children find one kind of supportive environment

---

3 Enlightenment is the ultimate goal of Buddhist practice. The Buddha searched for enlightenment, and when he reached it, he was called 'Thatagatha' which means 'the awakened one'. His intention was to share his wisdom with all other living beings, so they could wake up as well.

more helpful, and other children need different kinds of support. We have family members, pets, classmates, colleagues and friends. They are all there to help us learn to wake up. They are all there to motivate us to reach enlightenment. So we must realise that we are one of the motivators for our children, to help them reach tranquillity, wisdom and enlightenment, and develop clear minds.

Children and suffering

As a parent you may feel, 'I try to be a good parent, I give my children everything they desire, but they are still not happy. What will make them happy?' You don't really know what your child desires. What he wants is not what you want. Children's needs will never be satisfied by your buying them things all the time. What they want is *not* to get – it is to *give*. Your child may want to be a farmer – that is how he or she wants to contribute to the world. Without realising what harm we are doing, we stop that desire and make that child become a lawyer or an accountant. Be very careful that your children are not being forced to do what you want, rather than what *they* want. They need to be who they really are, to be able to give of themselves and find happiness in their own way.

What else will make your child happy? Children want to ask questions. You want them to be quiet. You want them to dress in a certain way. Parents demand instead of listening. Children want to express themselves, but parents ignore this need. We give our children what we think they need, and they're not satisfied because it's not what they *really* need. And one day, they forget what they need because they haven't been listened to – they have been stopped from being honest and intuitive. One day they give up, and hide their desires deep in their heart. Eventually they ask for the wrong things, because they have forgotten what the right things were, the things they really wanted and needed, deep down. They get these new things, the wrong things, and they are never satisfied, because they have forgotten what was really important to them.

You may have a child who is suffering at school. She is so unhappy. What can you do? You can only help your child if you are not *attached*[4] to that suffering. This is not to say you do not feel compassion. But if you are irritated, hurt, or consumed with pain from your child's suffering, you are

---

4 Attachment causes suffering. The more attached we are to things and people, the more painful our life is. Attachment is different from loving, caring and compassion. It contains emotions that cause us to desire things and hate things and act without thought. It is possible to care about ourselves and others without attachment, and this is one of the goals of Buddhism.

simply not able to be of help. If you can practice non-attachment you are no longer part of the child's unhappiness, you can see the problem for what it is, not what you think it is, where you mistake it as being the same as your own suffering or unhappiness. Don't add your own emotions into it. In this world, everyone has problems. But having problems doesn't stop you from finding happiness. You can be strong for others. If you are balanced, you don't have to suffer with others, or make yourself suffer in order to help people. If you are balanced, you don't have to change. So deal with your own sadness first. Become humble and empty, and listen to your child. When you are humble, you are not inviting other people's sadness with your sadness. Then you may find that the child's sadness may not really be there. If you are empty[5], you can deal with your child's sadness simply, not in a complicated way, overlaid with your own issues and problems.

Can you really help your children solve their problems? Not really. The best you can do is to stop causing problems for them. So you need to be at peace and have no anger. If we care and we are not sad, we will not trigger their sadness. You cannot live their lives for them. Let your children be. Let them be themselves. Be there for them, understand.

Discipline

Discipline is helpful for children, but right discipline is not "what I want you to learn" or "what I want you to do and say". Discipline that destroys the child's sense of self is harmful and brings resentment. Discipline for the child's personal growth, that helps the child find himself and develop inner calm will make a child feel safe and know that you love him. Children really do want discipline. But different discipline is needed for different mind states. Everyone has a different level of mental maturity. You may feel that you have the authority to reward and punish your child, but rewards and punishments bring resentment. You need to see your child's potential and use discipline to help bring out her potential. A little bit of a push provides children with the opportunity to develop. Discipline motivates us to achieve our potential. Discipline should provide the guidelines that help a child to grow up in the best way.

Discipline needs to be based on the *causes* of behaviour, not the *results*. You cannot stop an action without removing the cause of that action. That is the only discipline that is helpful. If a child is hitting others, he must have been hit first. Any symptom is informative. Don't suppress the symptoms.

---

5 *Emptiness is one of the three Dharma Seals which bring liberation from fear, confusion and sadness.*

They are the warnings to remove the cause. Stopping the symptoms just creates another problem. If your child fights against his brother, if you don't find out the cause of that fighting, one day he will fight in public. How do you think street fighters are created? How are killers created? No-one attended to their symptoms with compassion and gave them the correct discipline. If your child is stealing things, without getting to the cause of the stealing, punishment will push the cause underground. He may end up as an adult robbing a bank. Punishment for stealing and hitting kills the symptoms, but does not handle the cause. You find the cause with deep looking and deep listening.

Being with teenagers

As your child gets older, the issues seem to change. Many teenagers seem to have this strong craving for sex, drugs, alcohol and cigarettes. Physically congested bodies crave more and more. They are like crowded freeways, where there is no time or space to think, only to react. Decongestion is the only answer. This is discussed in chapter seven. This 'wanting' is from bad nutrition. We need to look at their diet, their physical and mental diet. Nourish your child with the right food, drink and thoughts. Contaminated[6] minds choose the wrong path. If your body is congested, you crave poison, like junk food, because your mind craves it. We will talk later about our relationship with food, but consumption is not only related to food, and contamination is not only related to the body. If you are hurting yourself, you will attract people who are hurting others. If you are not balanced, you will see enemies. Your teenager may be hurting, and in need of your calm attention. He may be looking for a way to break out of this cycle of craving, and not know how. What he needs is your deep listening and your deep caring.

If you are pure and clear, people are not 'others'. They are not 'friends' or 'enemies', they are you. You are other people. We are all inter-linked. A clear mind sees this and realises wisdom. Wisdom does not come from being taught. It comes from clarity of mind, being able to see the reality of existence.

Clarity of mind comes from your first family. Who helps you to have this purity of mind? It's your first family. They are your school, your hospital, your legal advice centre. They are everything to you. From the safety of your first home, you gradually expand to make the whole world your home. If you don't have a good foundation from your first family, you are

---

6 A contaminated mind is one that is overwhelmed with desires, dislikes and misconceptions. Following the five precepts and the eightfold path helps clear the mind.

going to leave this world empty-handed, unless you can learn from your friends, your work colleagues and find answers yourself, through your search for enlightenment.

The teenage years should be calm and happy for youngsters. If your teenagers are suffering, realise that these problems started much earlier. Young ones try to tolerate their lives, try to control their deep needs by suppressing them, not talking about them. One day it becomes too much. They can't take it any more. It becomes intolerable. We think it only happens in the teen years, but it starts much earlier. The child has been filling a trash can with his problems and needs and emotions, and then he can't fit any more in. The trash can is full. So it overflows. That's what you see, the overflowing of their emotions that cannot be managed. To feel more comfortable with these heavy burdens, they look for people with the same problems, the same emotions. It gives them strength to explode. That's how gangs are formed, as a way of acting out their pain.

But it is not too late. Be patient. It took ten or fifteen years to make the problem. Remember how long it took to create. So be patient. Understand. They will be touched by your patience and understanding, and you are one step closer to creating harmony between you. It is not from convincing, correcting, punishment, talking, and reasoning that they recover their sense of self. It is from your patience and emptiness that you help them recover. Be aware that everyone is important, every day. Every day is new. You will see hope because you will see change.

Relationships with your adult children

As your children grow into adults, they change. As parents we need to realise this. If you realise that your children mature, age, and develop different interests and life situations, you will also be aware that their needs change. See those changes, and learn. Let go of the past. Do not be attached to the past. You must realise that they and you have both changed. We all need to evolve. Remember that your children are not newborn, they are *reborn*. They are different now to how they were as children, because all of us are re-born and changing every moment. We all bring with us baggage from past experiences, mixed in with our current experiences. We get so caught up in things from the past that we are not totally aware of, that we stop looking at what's happening *now*. This new person, this grown-up child, is a mature adult. You need to see those changes so you don't hurt each other. You can no longer treat a grown-up adult as if he or she were a baby or school kid. If you do not let your relationship evolve into something new and relevant for today, you are building your own prison to enslave yourself, creating an illusion of suffering because you haven't let go of the past, and it will become worse and worse as you get older if you don't learn to let go.

As parents grow older

The first family is a powerful force in anyone's life. But not all first families are healthy or happy. As adults we are often faced with aging parents who seem to bring out the worst in us. How do we deal with this? Someone I know has a mother who is dying of cancer, and she is torn between her mother's needs and demands and her own needs. She says, "I feel I have responsibilities to my mother, who has a spinal tumour. But I want to move to another continent to pursue a new career (which my mother doesn't even know about). We have not really talked about what I am doing for a very long time. In fact I haven't seen her for ten years, until a few months ago, when my father died, and she developed cancer. I feel a sense of duty, but I don't even feel I love her. What can you advise?"

The truth is that we cannot really help others. We can only help ourselves. You can try to help through your kindness and wisdom, but she will have her own suffering. If you stay with her, her suffering will be in the pain of the disease. If you are not here, she will say, "My daughter left me!". Don't try to cheat yourself thinking, 'I'm here, I'm helping her. I shouldn't go away.' If you feel comfortable, go. The decision is up to you. If you don't feel comfortable, don't go. Do what makes you comfortable. We have our practice[7] wherever we go. When you go, you take your mom with you. Without your mom, you don't know how to care. Wherever you go you always have your family that you can love. I am not with my mom now. Other family members are with her on another continent. If you are not even living in the same town in this country, there is very little difference if you are on one continent or another. You can travel to reach her in a day from any other part of the world. Often we make ourselves feel guilty. We feel we should love our aged parents, but we don't. In this life we're not perfect. It's OK if we have some negative relationships. If you say all your relationships are perfect, you're fooling yourself. So if you live in a different town to your mother, you are already separated. Don't make it so complicated. *Loving self and loving others is the same thing.* If you do things for others without pleasure, they will feel you are upset and irritated and it won't help.

Sometimes we are taught that we must work at broken relationships and to try to fix them. But we need to avoid

---

7 One's practice is the moment by moment work of living a mindful life. It does not depend on one's surroundings or companions.

the challenge of such very painful emotions. Dealing with such extreme pain brings more defilement and contamination. Sometimes no matter how much you talk to someone, and try to understand him or her, you just can't. If I'm talking to you, and you understand, it means we are already on the same wavelength, and I'm not teaching you. You get it. We are in tune with each other. But spending time trying to change someone? No. Rather spend time doing what you think is right, what is good for your own personal growth. Find others who are easier to learn from.

We need to develop the habit of being with people and not discriminating between them. We develop this slowly, through our family and other relationships. And then, once we are enlightened, we can be with anyone, and not be disturbed by them. But until then, we need support as we slowly work towards understanding, letting go of the ego. We need to find the people who will bring out the beauty in us. Everybody has Buddha-nature, but we also have strong imprints from the past. If the family environment brings out the 'devil' in us, if it reminds us of the pain of the past, then we will end up fighting against each other, and everyone in the family will be destroyed. We don't need to punish ourselves like that.

Turning tragedy into happiness

The tragedy of this earth is that we have a love/hate relationship with things and people. We don't really know what real love is. Just because we are older and bigger than our children for the first decade or two of their lives, we may have treated our children in an uncaring way. That's why we have repeated problems over and over.

There is a way out of this endless suffering. The Buddhist way is a mindful way to live on this earth, not to escape to the Pure Land[8], but to create the Pure Land within. To be a mom or dad, a sister or brother, a daughter or son, a wife or husband, is to be in a human relationship. If you work hard as a mom or secretary or engineer, and you don't realise the purpose of that job is to find balance in yourself, you're missing a wonderful learning opportunity. We take on these roles to learn, to practise letting go, to find no self, no ego and a wholesome life. Any relationship provides the tools for us to learn to be at one with others. To develop a balanced mind, to be one with others, is our ultimate goal.

---

8 Pure Land is the place we find well-being, joy and serenity. It is a place of perfection.

Friends

Friends

There can be some misunderstanding about what a friend is. Only those people helping us find an easier route to insight and understanding, those people who help bring out the beauty within us, are our true friends. Sometimes people think, 'If I have friends, I will have a harbour of love to support me, my problems will be solved, my life will be full!' Sorry, no.

Our friends are individuals who have a very similar status to us. We are easily affected by our own environment - we're not in control. The environment will bring up what we have in us, arouse our emotions, and push our buttons. But our friends easily accept us as we are, because we are like them. We will not easily arouse their discrimination or criticism or anger. They will not try to control or change us.

Whenever we feel that people are trying to control us, we quickly spring to our own defence. That does not help us grow. People try and teach us, point out where we are wrong, but we defend ourselves. We jump to our own defence and react in negative ways. This only makes us more darkened, defiled, and congested. The do-gooders mean well, but do harm, because they trigger our ego. Our friends don't do that. Our friends will be those people who accept us and bring out the beauty in us, instead of that strong ego. They may have the same difficulties we do, but they allow us to be ourselves. They are connected to us. They accept us. With them, we are willing to not hide things, but to be open, to share and support each other, so our friends bring connectedness to us. If your mom did not help to bring out your beauty as a child, you will turn somewhere else – maybe to your dog, because the dog helps bring out your beauty in your caring for him. A retired man may make friends with a dog because it allows him to bring out his caring and support. Even a tree can serve the purpose of being a friend.

A child has a need to be loved, respected and accepted and then the child will learn to love. Love is not the action of the ego to defend or offend. That's not love. In the presence of love we don't have to pretend, hide or overdo it. We just have to be who we are, sincere and honest. That is love. So love comes from a pure mind. If I hear someone say, "I love someone – it's so painful!" that's not love. Love will never bring pain. We should distinguish between *pure love* and *self-love*. Pure love means *no self*. It means inter-being, where the other is part of us, and we are part of them. You are with people and you accept them, you are there for them, they do not offend or hurt you or defend their own ego. That is what friendship is about – caring for others while we learn to find the beauty in ourselves.

Our first family helps us to build the most important bonds we will make in this life. The people in our first family affect us as newborn babies and they support and love us. If our first family is happy and supportive, we don't need to search for support elsewhere. Often our search for friends is really to find a remedy for the need that was never satisfied in our first family.

Before we look at all the roles friends fill, let's think about the young child's gradual development. For the child, the first family is 'just people'. Everybody needs people. We don't have to discriminate. Anyone can provide a human relationship to fill the need in us. The newborn needs to be in good hands, and the first family is supposed to care the most. They need to be attentive. Sadly, sometimes these people are not caring and concerned. It's not that they don't want to be concerned. It's just that they don't know how. They are insensitive because they are not enlightened. They are not able to live moment by moment. They are not attentive. This problem creates a need in the child. He needs to go out and make friends, hoping that he will get the support for which he longs.

Mothers and fathers have been programmed genetically to make strong attachments to their offspring. They are programmed to feel, 'This child is mine; other children are not mine'. So this programming makes it easier for the mother and father to practice giving to the child and to provide a good role model of love and caring behaviour. In fact, parents feel guilty if they are not loving and caring towards their family. This burden of guilt makes it easier for them to practice kindness to family members, because there is so much pressure from society and from our genes to do so. Whether we admit it or not, society frowns on people who desert or neglect or harm their children. This forced incentive makes us build the relationship with our child whether we want to or not.

As children, we watch and learn from our mothers and fathers, and see their habit of giving to us, sharing with us, caring for us and protecting us. We copy what we see. After we have built this habit of giving love, we can apply this behaviour to others outside the family more easily.

Learning about friendship from our first family

One mistake we make in our first family is that we learn to discriminate. We distinguish between people who are 'family' and 'not family'. We think, 'You are my brother'. 'You are *not* my brother'. So that leaves a huge group of people that we don't include in our lives and in our relationships.

Sometimes, when we talk about 'friends' we show we are discriminating. We imply that 'you *are* my friend', and 'you are *not* my friend'. Others are not friends. They are not family. They are excluded. We need to build our relationships with friends, so that eventually we can extend our friendship to include everyone. We start learning how to do this within our first family. If they're not there for us, we look for friends to help us learn this vital lesson. We need this practice.

In the first family, we tend to see our mother and our father in particular roles. They are the ones who give us discipline, reward us, that kind of thing. Sometimes their love is conditional, based on our behaviour. If you behave in this way, you will be treated better or rewarded by your mother or father. If you behave in that way, you will be punished or excluded. This is how we are socialised. In the family, you will learn that people are different. Family relationships do tend to teach us discrimination. Here is my father: I have to behave with him in a certain way, and speak in a certain way that he finds acceptable. But I can be different with my mother, and different again with various brothers, sisters, cousins, and even aunts and uncles. I learn a different way to relate to each of them. And I also learn that if this person is my mother, all the others are 'not mother'. So I learn discrimination.

Why we need friends

This discrimination has drawbacks for our personal growth. We have now excluded the large majority of people in our minds, because they are 'not family'. So we need to learn that even if people are 'not family' they can still be part of us. Happily, there are people outside the family who can help in this personal growth. Friends help one to learn how to give, and how to care. We are all on this planet to help each other. The individual can learn about kindness from his friends; from giving he becomes connected with other people. From the experience of having friends, we learn to be kind and concerned about others outside the family. So we learn first from our family and then from our friends, and then we are able to extend this wisdom to all our other relationships. Friends have this most important role – they help us to learn how to give. Friends will teach the individual how to give and how to be touched and connect with people. We learn from friendship to be able to extend that caring towards another person outside of the family, so that we can be in touch with anyone and become whole and complete.

Making friends

Why do I find it difficult to make friends? Let's say I have an unsatisfactory first family, what do I do if I haven't learned the skills to make friends, to be at ease with others?

Sometimes in the first family, the child picks up narrow-minded ideas about relationships. The first family can teach a child that outside people (who are not family members) are not to be trusted, that they are 'the bad guys'. Parents warn us: "Don't be friends with them." That kind of fear of the outside environment makes it difficult to make friends, and encourages people to withhold their trust of others. They see people who are not part of the family as something to fear, to be wary of. They think people outside the family will hurt or harm them. The family talks about bad experiences with so-called friends, so children develop a fear of outsiders beyond the home. Only the family feels safe. In the same way, other people from other families have the same fears, and have also been given the wrong idea that because you are not related to them by blood, you are not a caring person. So it works both ways, both in us and in others.

So we feel our family will care for us (in whatever way they can), and sometimes we also learn that when we go out into the world we will have to compete with, suppress and overpower others in order to survive.

Another reason a child can find it difficult to make friends is that the child is spoiled in the first family. The child has been negatively wanting people to care and love and support him. He may have been given no opportunity to practice feeling other people's needs and seeing their point of view, and may never have learned how to be considerate. These children expect everyone to serve them. You have to break through this barrier of expecting everything and giving nothing, in order to make friends.

So, if people can allow these walls between them to collapse, they can be brought together so that friends will feel just as good as family. We can at last move beyond this idea that friends and family are different, because underneath, they are not.

Assets from the past

If we don't have mentors, good, kind, wise role models to show us how to behave with love and concern for others, it is very difficult for us to grow and mature.

It is often difficult to avoid learning wrong lessons from the first family. As Buddhists, we believe that everybody is born with assets, with strong good habits, from the past. We believe that you don't necessarily have to pick up behaviour from your immediate family. As a child you can also teach them. Sometimes the children in the family are the role models, the wise ones. Think of the alcoholic parent whose children have to be mature while he or she is drunk and out of control. The sad thing is that sometimes a child who brings wisdom with him is forced to change to match the aberrations of the family. Children have no authority. So sometimes, children are confused. They come with openness, but their parents overpower them, demand discipline, and make them follow and obey rules that don't make any sense. Sometimes a child will develop two personalities, one he shows to friends and the other for the family. Two different selves. These children may have great past knowledge but are not allowed to show it at home.

You have probably seen different children within the same family. One may be shy and withdrawn, and the other outgoing and sociable. With strong roots from the past, a child will find it easier to make friends. Why is it that a person will have bad family relationships but great friends? Because he has a strong background from the past, and his natural behaviour comes out again with his friends, away from the suppression of a mixed-up first family. If a child in an unhappy first family does not have a strong past life background, he or she is doomed. You bring your looks from the past. You see how beautiful some babies are. They are showing their character and deeds from before. Everyone has 20 years to change their looks this lifetime. So if your looks change as you grow to be an adult, you have to accept responsibility, because these changes are based on your current behaviour this lifetime, on what you do. So babies are born with past merits. That's why they are so beautiful. Then their current actions will affect the way their faces develop this time around.

If the first family didn't allow their child to be caring, they will create a spoilt child. So as parents, we need to remember all the time that we should allow and encourage our children to feel for others, and do things to help others. We need to teach our children how to reach out if they don't know how. So, if things go well, the first family teaches the child how to reach out, break the ice and build friendships.

Earned and forced relationships

There are many differences between the relationship with a friend and the relationship with family members. The relationship with friends is an *earned* one, not a *forced* one. We will separate from our family one day. We won't always stick with certain groups. The first group teaches us how to be with people. Then we move on to make friends at school, at work, in our sports or social clubs and activities. But it's the first family that teaches us how.

One natural fact of life is that humans tend to stick together. Whatever we do, we are almost forced to be with other people. The hermit or loner is an exception to the normal social patterns of humans. So we will always associate with people wherever we go. And if your first family did right by you, wherever you go you will find friends. It will be easy.

Letting go

Sometimes we miss our friends and our family. Because life is change, circumstances take us to different places and different occupations. When we start missing our friends, we are learning a new lesson. We are being prepared to be 'at home' with all sorts of people. We slowly learn to feel that we are not alone, no matter where we are. We start to see that we don't have to go back to our home town to feel we have friends or family. If we have a strong attachment to particular friends and family members we will be very miserable. We need the skill to be with all sorts of people wherever we are, to know that they are not strangers, not enemies, but part of us.

We learn from the first easy relationships, and move on to the later, more difficult ones. Eventually, we will realise that we are even 'in relationship' with the other drivers on the freeway. We are surrounded by friends, even if we're not aware of it.

Choosing friends

How can I meet the right people who will become my friends? How should I choose my friends? Let's think about this. What is meant by the 'right' people? For your personal growth, the right people for you are the ones that will motivate you to give, to open up, to share and to support others. They will make you more positive in connecting with other people. Good friends give you more, and they make you give more as well, they energise you to give, share and support others. Now be careful about this definition – good people are not people who 'do good'. They are those who motivate *you* to do good. The reason is that no matter how good or bad your friend is, if he can help you feel joy in doing good, in helping *him*, he is a valuable friend to have. A good person can help you to be like him. He should help you to see him as he is, to see inside him. He needs also to help bring the beauty out of you, so you can see his beauty. The best friend is a person who has purified him or herself, who has let go of ego, let go of self. These friends have no attachment. Their minds are clear and their hearts are open. Only when your mind is clear and your heart is open will you feel joyful, glad, energetic and whole. Who will help you to do that? Your good friends, the right friends for you. If any relationship makes you feel closed, possessed, greedy, narrow-minded, or selfish, be wary. That kind of relationship breaks you. You are not energised by it, you are drained.

As you start working towards becoming a more fulfilled, enlightened person, choose your friends carefully. The right friends will let you share the joy of letting go, of being yourself, of hiding nothing, of reaching out, without expecting anything in exchange. They will encourage you to love. Your husband should also be your friend. Your wife should be your friend. Your children are your friends, because they help you to become complete and whole.

You need to find the right people to energise you. They help you find the energy to build the right habits. So the right habits become part of you, they become effortless practice. It is said that you can change a habit in as little as six weeks. We unknowingly build wrong habits in our lives, and then have to work very hard to change them later. It is easier and wiser to choose to practice the right habits first time. The kind of friends we choose either help or hinder us in building healthy ways of behaving. And over time, the ways we have chosen to behave become effortless. This is what we mean by effortless practice. So in order to have the energy to change harmful practices (like giving up smoking), you need to make an effort, and to do that, you need support. If every one of your relationships is tough, you're going to drain your energy and it will be very difficult to change your behaviour, even if you know it's harming you and others. So friends can be a major support in building good practice, in practicing the right ways of behaving, the ways that we know are humanitarian, life-affirming and positive.

Initially, you get energised by your family. You go to school, and people drain you. Then you have to go back to your family and friends to recover and be energised again. It's the same when you go to work. You need to come back to a safe place and loving people where you can be yourself, rest and recover. We can move beyond this need to be re-energised by family and friends, until one day we don't feel drained any more. That's our mission in life. *Our mission is not to find the best friends, but to grow so that anyone can be our friend.* Then you can be with any kind of person without being drained. You will then be able to discard the idea of having to discriminate between different groups, and having to choose who to be with and who to avoid. In reality, you need to have lots and lots of groups to connect with. If you have only a few groups, you will become too attached and then when they are not with you, you will be so lonely.

Are some friends really friends?

What about the friend who lets us down? How do we deal with that? Why do friends behave in that way? First, we need to get rid of the idea that a friend will let us down. Your friend didn't let you down. You just didn't know him. You have a version of your friend in your head and you are disappointed when the real person is different from what you thought he was. But this only happens because you don't really know the reality. You have the wrong notion of your friend, your own limited conception. You have expectations that you make up from your dreams and imaginings.

People are the way they are. One friend talks a lot about everything, to everyone. That is her 'suchness', the way she is. To expect her to be silent, to be what she is not, is to have false expectations. When you see the reality of your friend, and understand her, you will never be disappointed. You create a problem for yourself if you have expectations. The loved one will become a hated one. You will only turn relationships sour if you have expectations. So avoid expectations.

How do you get to know your friends? To a large extent, you choose who you are comfortable with. You create your friends. Who your friends are is who you are. If your friends seem like monsters, you have a monster in you. If you see your friend as gentle, it's like a mirror. If there is no impurity in you, you will know your friend for who he or she is, and you will find pure friends.

The defiled[1] mind

Sadly, almost all of us have unexplored issues, prejudices, false ideas, fears, hates, cravings and delusions. We call this the defiled mind. The more defiled our minds are, the more we will choose friends who reflect the same defilements. We are comfortable with them. So you, with a defiled mind, a congested mind, filled with all this unexamined stuff, you create another you in your friends. We are impure. We create other impure people out of this impurity. But if we are empty here inside, we see others as they are, we see the

---

[1] The defiled mind can also be called the obscured or congested mind. It is another word for ignorance, the unexamined false thinking that blocks our understanding the true nature of existence. Buddhists hold that this ignorance is the root cause of all human suffering.

reality. If you have standards inside you, you judge the person by your standards. The person is impure due to *your own* defilements within you.

Let us take another example. I am seen as a different person by a hundred others. Each of these hundred people will see a different me in front of them. Because each of them views me through a filter of his own thoughts, attachments, past experiences, cravings, aversions and errors of thinking. Only an enlightened being will see me as I am. So your friends are great teachers. Whatever you see in them is something in yourself that needs attention and healing.

Few friends, many friends ...

Those who have many friends have fewer attachments. They are easily able to treat people as who they are, and allow them to be themselves. They will not try to control them. They have more respect for others. Their friends are allowed to be other people's friends. They make fewer demands on their friends and they show them more respect.

If you are short of friends, you probably are very attached to the ones you have. So you don't let them go. You ask, "Why don't they call? What are they doing now? Why don't they visit me?" You cling to them. You try and contain them and hold them tightly. A person with many friends allows those friends to lead their own lives. They have fun when they are together and do not limit each other. They also don't say, "This is my friend, this is *not* my friend". If you have many friends, you are more confident and happy in yourself, more able to live your life one moment at a time.

Good friends are not like baggage, always hanging around like a briefcase or a handbag. Good friends are not like your shadow. They give you space. They do not govern you. Those that have few friends are scared to lose them, they do not know how to have a free, relaxed relationship.

So how can you change from having few friends to having many? First, let people see you as you are, don't put up barriers and pretend to be someone else. Then, accept others as they are. If you find it difficult to accept a friend as he or she is, if you react to their behaviour, if you react with strong emotion to things your friends do, you need to examine yourself. Everyone creates their own world. If you experience unacceptable behaviour in others, this becomes a form of guidance to look inside yourself.

False friends

Some people who are powerful or wealthy have the problem of appearing to attract 'friends' who may not be genuine. Why are some people friends because of what I *have* rather than who *I am*?

It's good to be wanted, even if it's for your money or power. Everyone needs to be wanted. It feels good to be given attention, to be liked. If you want to be my friend because I have the right possessions, it will only bother me because I am not strong. The thing is, are we strong enough in ourselves to make friends and keep friends even if we don't have the money, the possessions or the power? We will only feel resentful of people 'using' us if we feel we are not worthy without our wealth, if our wealth is all we see of value about ourselves. Everyone enjoys being of service to others. Helping others with our wealth and power is a valuable thing to do. There is nothing to fear in doing that. So there is no reason why we should feel bad about helping people or allowing people to benefit from our power or strength, or judge them harshly because they do so.

Remember that when 'bad' people use you for their own benefit, this creates their own defilement. They are the problem, not you. They damage themselves by using you in this way. Even though you are being abused by them, they are the ones who are harmed. It may be some comfort to know that they are harmed by their own behaviour. However, if you reject them or judge them, you will then defile yourself. So be careful how you treat those supposed 'users and abusers' *Your* actions are what you in the end must be accountable for, not theirs. Once you start thinking, 'They are so greedy, so two-faced, they are using me', your own thoughts will defile you. It's their responsibility to improve their minds, not yours. So how do you respond then? You should not be bothered by them, but you have to be responsible for how you see them. If you see them as greedy or as using you, it's your problem. It doesn't really matter what they say and think about you. That is not the issue. It's what you say and think about them that will have consequences.

We can use these people around us to learn about ourselves. They are our guardians and our protectors because they help us to become complete, to see our attachments and to learn to let go. Their actions can purify us if we know how to bring this beauty out of us. We don't have to feel responsible for other people's impurity. That's their own homework. We cannot clean up for them.

When our friends suffer ...

Sometimes we have friends who need help, who are struggling, who are suffering difficulties in life. Where does our responsibility towards our friends begin and end?

How can we help our friends? We can't. We are not the creators of others. We can only accept them as they are – by being patient and being there for them. That is helping them to not bring out their limitations. All people have some darkness within them. Most people who say they want to help others have in reality been trying to push, convert, change or discipline them. This attention to other people's faults brings out even more negative energy from the dark parts of the mind. Just to be there for your friends is being helpful.

To be helpful, we must be humble. When a friend cries, "Help!" we often respond by being super-helpful. "This is what *I* can do to help you!" No, that is not the way. They have their own pace. Maybe it takes long years for them to de-programme the problems they are facing. Maybe it will take more than one life for them to learn whatever lesson is facing them.

Good people can be so arrogant. We need to realise that we can't push people to change. As long as you are not judgemental, as long as you are patient and understanding, and see them as they are, you are helping, because they are not pushed and they are not judged. If, on the other hand, you *do* help them, you make them feel inferior, useless. They become so depressed because they think they cannot meet your requirements. They feel they cannot repay you for what you have given them. So you make them weaker rather than stronger. Humans don't do the work of changing others. Not even God does that work. If God hasn't changed that person, what makes us think that we will be able to? We have been granted the gift of choice. We have to allow others to choose whether or not to work on changing themselves. Not to allow people to do their own growing is disrespectful. Love becomes hate because we do not respect people. Sometimes so-called love is linked to trying to control or judge the ones you say you love. When they are obedient, following you, delivering your needs, you love them, and when they don't you hate them. That's not really love.

The balance between friends and family

Why is it that so often, husbands can't stand their wife's friends, or wives want to change, ignore or exclude their husband's friends? Sometimes parents don't like a child's friends. Friends can sometimes cause problems in relationships with our family members. Some people feel that their wife or husband or parent dislikes their friends, even if nothing is ever said or done. What can be done in this unhappy situation where our friends are not welcome in our home, or we are uncomfortable about the friends our family members associate with?

The truth is that all your negative feelings towards the other family member's friends are buried in you already. You don't know about those feelings, you probably hide them or deny them, until certain conditions arise, then the emotions arise. Once the condition or circumstances or environment arises (like the presence of some person in our home doing or saying something that offends us), only then do we see what is in our mind, what emotional reaction we have hidden deep down. This person, this circumstance gives the family an excuse to bring up that feeling.

What do we do? Our family may not know this friend. Parents and other family members probably have not had frequent communications or heart-to-heart talks with this person, so they can be scared, frightened or have other emotions. How can they have such strong feelings for a stranger? What they are really saying is "I don't like the way you make friends. I don't like you." But they pick on our friends instead of on us. We have to ask our parents or loved one to be honest about what is in their own mind, and listen deeply.

Friends of loved ones

If you really accommodate your wife or husband, you will accommodate their friends. If you love your children you will welcome their friends, because those people are what your children need.

If you judge your daughter's friend as unfit, that means your daughter is also unfit. And if your daughter is unfit, of course she will choose unfit friends. Your daughter's friends are chosen by her own needs and the way she is. If you love your daughter, how can you *not* love your daughter's friends? Rejecting your daughter's choice, rejecting your daughter's friends, is not going to solve the problem. Your daughter and her friends will go away, and meet elsewhere. She will hide from you inside. She could mess up her life without you there. You need to let your daughter's friends be in your home, in your sight. Your daughter may leave these friends and choose other unwanted friends. You cannot separate the shadow from your daughter. Love your daughter. Accept your daughter. Accept her decisions. Accept her friends. Your daughter will be safe if you open up to awaken her, and give her the blessing of your wisdom. Otherwise your worry will always be there. Your daughter's friends are your daughter's duplicates. Because she is searching for herself, looking for people she can identify with.

Some people find their life partner's friends boring or unpleasant, too noisy, too quiet, too rough, or too stuck up. It's amazing how many things can be wrong with our husband's and wife's friends. How do we solve this problem?

The problem exists because we have a certain way of thinking. 'I have to make friends with my husband's friends, my children's friends'. No, you don't. It's impossible. Everyone is so different. You have 'your' version of your husband. And others have their own versions of him. We need to allow each other space to have different versions, different understandings of others. We all live in the same world, but have different needs. We have our own interests and hobbies. Your husband's friends may bring out different sides of him, and give him pleasure in ways that you can't. His friends are *right for him*. You can't govern them or know everything in their minds. You may think 'I cannot include this friend of my husband's because I don't like him. My husband shouldn't make friends with him.' If you have this need to control, it means that part of you is incomplete. There is no space in you. Give your husband space and you will have space. If you control your husband, he will control you. If you want others to give you space, they must have space from you. Your resentment will invite your husband's resentment. Maybe your husband will be accommodating, but will hide his resentment. Sooner or later, the emotion will come out. It then becomes a family problem, and there will be arguments and fights. If you are going to choose your husband's friends for him, you are in the cycle of suffering. If you hate other people's friends, you are in the loop of suffering.

Unwanted approaches from friends

Sometimes friends of other family members can create problems in the family. How does one respond to a friend's husband or wife who makes sexual advances to you? You may be shocked, but may also be flattered. But regardless of your feelings, you need to make some sort of response. What do you do when the bounds of friendship change, and the relationship starts to change?

One of the greatest dangers today is the lack of control that adults show in their sexual behaviour towards people who are already sexually committed. When people have that kind of unhealthy thought, this is the mutual responsibility of the friend and the spouse that is being approached. It's not only the friend's problem, it's yours too. It's because you unconsciously invite that kind of care and support from your friend, because you are not self-reliant. You are sad, lonely, hurt, in need. Maybe you don't ask for it but you send out unspoken messages inviting that kind of comfort from people. If you are self-reliant, there will be no gap to invite that kind of response. We are ignorant. Sometimes we don't realise our thoughts send out messages all the time. We are so insecure and troubled and insensitive that we don't know what we are doing. We are surprised, humiliated and angry when we have that kind of approach. You might send out that message – you want attention and support from your husband – but the message goes out to your friends as well. Your friend wants to 'deliver the order' you have sent out. But if you didn't let it out, there would be no one there responding, showing it back to you, reflecting it, because they got the message. You need instead to examine how you can enrich your relationship with your husband, so your needs are fulfilled, or work on your own personal development and learn how to love yourself.

Demanding friends

I have friends who demand a lot of my time and energy – more than I want to spare. What should I do with such demanding friends?

Weak people will be demanding. They will be greedy. They will lean on you because you allow them to do so. We think, 'Through my time spent with them, they will be fine!' You think you are the angel, the protector, the guardian, the teacher. You think that with a few meetings they will become different people. Well, that's impossible. If you have that expectation, you will be irritated. Your plan for them is, 'They're going to be fine now'. You think you have saved them already! But they keep coming back and *that is not the plan!* You find it annoying, but that annoyance is because you are disappointed in yourself, not in them, because you over-estimate yourself, and you under-estimate the problem. You are suffering from delusions. You have been giving them the message that you are the only answer, that you are their eternal support. You need to let them know they have to run their lives themselves. If you give them the message that you are the only answer, they will depend on you only. If they know that support comes from within themselves, they will be patient and know you are not the answer. We invite those problems to come back to us.

Learning from our friends

When we can calmly observe our friends, we can learn a lot from them. How would we use our relationships with friends as a learning experience? Well, say we have friends who are behaving a certain way – say they are clinging to us. We can observe this, notice it, and see if we have similar behaviour. If I see behaviour reflected in someone close to me, it could be in me as well. If you can accept him as he is, there is no defilement in you causing you to hate him or like him for how he behaves or what he has done. We can be aware of something in another, but if it doesn't bring out an emotional reaction in us, then we don't have that defilement in ourselves. If that awareness doesn't bring another action – say you are aware of your friend's 'faulty' action, say their nature of clinging, or of greed, or aggression, if this doesn't bring any reaction from you, any emotional response, if it does not bother you, then there is no lesson there for you to learn. If you are detached about it, you are seeing them as they are. But if that behaviour in them irritates or annoys you, and causes you to react, then you can take that as a warning light. You can say to yourself, "Uh, oh, I am reacting very emotionally to Joe's need to control me. Let me examine this need to control others. Do I have some of that in myself? Where and when have I shown this kind of behaviour? What can I do to heal this in myself?"

Chapter 3

Relationships
at work

Relationships at Work

As adults, we all have to make a living or somehow share responsibility for our own survival in this world. We spend many years in preparation for this, so we can earn an income, support ourselves and others, and help the world. After we have built our professional skills, most of us have to undertake some sort of work for the major part of our lives.

The purpose of work

In Buddhism we talk about right livelihood. As Venerable Thich Nhat Hanh says, "The way you support yourself can be an expression of your deepest self, or it can be a source of suffering for you and others"[1]. Clearly some ways of earning a living violate ideals of love and compassion. Dealing in weapons, the slave trade, prostitution... how can these be right livelihood? On the other hand it is wonderful to have a vocation that benefits humans, animals, plants, and the earth. But sometimes jobs are hard to find. How do we balance the need to work with the need to live mindfully? How do we handle the relationships that arise in the workplace? How do we turn our work from being a punishment into being a source of calm and well-being for ourselves and others?

Potential and preparation

Everybody has different potential. If you can develop your special talents according to your potential, you will enjoy your work. Everybody contributes according to their potential. Their job arises from their commitment to this shared responsibility.

Money as a reason to choose a job

Sadly, most of us don't find joy in our work. We are misinformed, thinking that money is the only source of happiness. We think, 'If I am rich I will enjoy a good life.' With this misconception, we can choose work that does not bring us joy. Do you want to be a doctor or an engineer; do you want to work with plants, people, animals

---

[1] In his book, The Heart of the Buddha's Teaching (1988). New York: Broadway Books.

or computers? Everyone has different needs, but material matters control people. People think that money will create miracles in their lives.

What do long years of study bring?

People go to school, study further, get a degree. But learning is not the same as *realising* knowledge. You are acquiring knowledge, collecting it. When you are collecting it, you don't get much joy from that knowledge – it's just to be used in future. Your focus is on the future, you are looking at graduating, getting a job, accumulating power and money. Your wishes won't be fulfilled till much later. That knowledge has not yet helped you at school, so you are frustrated. You are not able to realise your knowledge by using it now, in the present.

When we are little, every action we do gives us satisfaction right away. We take joy in riding our bicycle, in climbing a wall, in balancing on a tree branch, in dressing our doll, in running on the grass. Young children really know how to live fully, in the moment. At school, we are often forced to study things that have no meaning for us, for which we can't see an immediate value. If throughout your education, you have to wait till later for future satisfaction, you will have more disappointment when you grow older. But if you can build up that satisfaction all the time, studying what you enjoy and value, doing practice and homework that is useful and has meaning for you, if you can do your school work and studies without resentment, every action becomes peaceful. That's a good foundation for the real world of work, and dealing with colleagues.

Sometimes we are lucky enough to study skills that satisfy us. If you enjoy music, then while you are practising it, you are fulfilled. If you are feeling pleasure while you write your school essays, you are enjoying using your writing skills. You don't need a book at the end of the effort. The pleasure is in the effort. It's not often that students can enjoy their studies as they are doing them. This is very sad.

When you are a student, you are told much of the time what is allowed, what is required, and how you should be. As students, we are not often consulted about our studies, we are simply told what to learn. It is not our choice, it's what society wants us to do. People believe that education will bring success. But studying for many years before working, one is misled into looking for something that will make one feel successful in the future. We wait for twenty years to feel successful, to feel recognised and respected. People don't realise this, and they don't enjoy the process of going through school and university, because they are not able to live in the present: their minds are stuck in the future.

As people develop their professional skills, they can also develop a hard heart, because they have been waiting so long. They have become insensitive to what's happening now. After they get their position, their power, they won't even notice they have arrived. They become more ambitious and greedy. They put their attention on being even more successful in future. During their whole life, they never get that peace of mind that comes from living in the present, because they are always looking for that future dream to come true.

In this social system it seems as though everybody has been programmed. Studying is to prepare us for work. We forget that studying is also a job. It's learning to be with people, with teachers, with classmates. People think that working in the home is not a job, working at school is not a job, and that the only jobs of any value are ones that involve working in an office. Clearly, that's not right.

Getting the high-status job

This gets even sadder. Because they have waited so long, and now finally have achieved a high status, working people can become arrogant. They become 'adult' so they have someone they can abuse, just as they were abused. All the way through their extended education they were waiting for adults to recognise and respect them. So they have been deeply hurt, and without thinking, they want others to suffer what they did. They do it to the next generation. They see their children as stupid, foolish, immature, just as they were seen when they were kids. They abuse their colleagues, look down on those under them. Their accumulation of emotion has become almost beyond control – it's as if they now have a licence to hurt and harm.

When working people are younger, they still have room to hide these emotions deep inside. But as they get older, these painful emotions fill them and bubble out. Working people can become arrogant. They lose the 'gentle heart' - the desire to be kindly and unwilling to hurt, harm or resent others. It's as if they finally get the licence to express their emotions, and all the bad ones come out. Now they are more senior they will control their subordinates. They may judge, discriminate between people, and have unsatisfactory relationships in the office. They can 'play mean' because they have been taught they are outsiders. The lesson they have learned over the years of waiting is that people have to be competed with, cheated on and overpowered. They feel they have to do whatever is necessary to get the rare opportunity, because their colleagues at work are not their family, and they don't have to love them. Being a successful executive can have the cruel side effect of making you cold-hearted, mean and rejecting.

Working for the future, working in the now

In this modern world, because you seem to be judged by your performance, your possessions and your position, you feel that those are the values of life. Most of time you are not balanced, because most of the time you are working at your goal to own those things. So you think only of the future, and you forget to live in the present. Maybe once in your lifetime, you feel, 'Oh, I am satisfied". But it has taken twenty or thirty years to get to that point. The short pleasure is not worth the years of pain.

People are often driven by future goals. You have a project, you need to accomplish this project, and it will take three years. For those three years you are so intense, so pressured. It's not worth it. It takes three years to get your Ph D. You are so worried all that time, so anxious. It's not worth it. You decide to raise money for the poor, and you work towards that goal for ten years. You are so concerned about the project. It's not worth it. People don't understand that any work is for peace of mind in the moment. *Peace of mind in the moment.* If we don't realise that, if we feel we have to move from one stage to another stage to get satisfaction, that is not the right way to work. You work eight hours, then you want to rest, because your work is so hateful to you. Or you work five days, then you need two days' holiday. That doesn't satisfy you, because you bring your stress and your pressure to your holiday. You bring your emotions back home. So all your time you are being haunted, possessed and defiled by the emotions your work generates in you, and that's not good. *Enjoy your work as you do it, in the now.* Enjoy the process and the results will happen naturally.

Pushing to get ahead

Working people rely on their salary to support their needs – they have to go to work, they have to be there. They hate the place, but they feel they cannot leave. They are greedy for the money, the money pays for their wants. But because the job they are doing was not chosen by them - it was chosen for the money and the power - the work is empty. This is so sad.

There is an executive position available at work. Everyone wants it. Why? Everyone wants to be the boss.

There's only one boss, so you fight for it, you try to take down those staff closest to you, so that you can have the job for yourself. Think about those hours in the office, how much emotion people are going to build up during the week, only to release it all when they get home. So they have the degree, the workplace appointment, the money – and a divorce. Of course they will have marriage problems, when the burdens at work are so extreme.

The right to live gracefully[2]

What we have forgotten is that *we all have the right to live gracefully in this world*. We have an obligation to make this world more beautiful, and we contribute according to our potential. If your job brings you satisfaction and a sense of fulfilment, it's more than money can bring you. With this kind of realisation then, the work environment can become a pleasant one, like the family relationship. Otherwise, with hate and fear, you'll be feeling rejected all the time by your colleagues. There will be cheating, jealousy, suspicion. If you don't know how to cleanse yourself of all this hate, fear and anger, finally you will drown in that negative energy within you that you are not even aware of.

In the beginning, you think you hate your boss, and the work people around you. Then gradually you start to hate yourself, you feel lost and confused. Why are you so unbalanced? It's because you have waited so long to become happy. In the end, even though you are aged 40, 50 or 60, and are rich and powerful, you are not happy at all. Your mother and father are not with you, your friends are busy in other parts of the country or the world, and you are left with only the people in the workplace. You miss your friends and your family. Life feels so empty.

Remember when we graduate from school, college or university, we are about to be separated from our loved ones. We will probably move out of our family home and live on our own. We will probably also lose touch with many of our friends, as they move away and find other jobs. If we don't prepare ourselves to make friends wherever we go, when we start work that loneliness will become a serious problem. That problem will affect our working life. We will be surrounded by lots of cold people with hardened hearts, who do not care about us. If we don't have friends and family to support us then, we will have a very unhappy working life, no matter how grand the car and house, no matter how great the power and money, because

---

[2] *Right action and right livelihood are part of the Noble Eightfold Path. See chapter 10.*

we have had to harm ourselves in order to get them. In order to resolve this pain, we need to think about right action and right livelihood.

Right actions towards right livelihood

Looking at the idea of right livelihood, we may be tempted to force ourselves into doing things that we are not yet ready for. We may choose a job because we think it will make us a better person. Don't try to become a good person. Don't try to do good things. If you have this kind of concept you could easily fall into the 'discrimination' trap. Instead of seeing all people as valuable, you set yourself up as being noble and good, and discriminate among people, judging some harshly, and this is not a good thing. You may start thinking: 'You are bad. I am good'. You become more arrogant because you are doing 'good' work and others are not.

Becoming connected at work

Most people work. They want to have a job to do. The risk at work is how the job is done. One's mind can be defiled by manipulating people - using them in a calculated way to get the job done. People may think this is their mission. 'I need to do this in order to make a profit and keep the business going'. They don't understand the real purpose of work is for us to meet others, to bring us together with others. The job takes effort, and keeps us busy doing things, but the essence of the work is for us to see *what is inside of us*. Because of this job, because of working with people, I might see my *defilements*. What are defilements? They are those ignorant thoughts and actions that stop us reaching wisdom. They are the things that hold us back and cause us pain and unhappiness. So any work that does not help us to become better connected with people, so we can grow in wisdom is not the right livelihood for us.

Causing all kinds of harm

Then there is the aspect of what you are producing in your work. What is your product or service? If I have to produce a product which is going to cause people to become more greedy, to want to possess, to own, or to feel hurt if they can't afford to have it, or if I have to force myself and others to work in an efficient way that makes people very stressed, and makes them feel inferior, that is not a good working environment for me or the people I work with, and that is not right livelihood.

Nowadays at the supermarket we see thousands of different products. How many do we really need in our household? Do we really need most of these things in our daily life? Not necessarily. So lots of supposedly successful business men – who are rich and important, and very professional and skilful - are actually cheating themselves, thinking, 'Oh I am successful because I have such a high position, such an accumulation of money, I hire thousands of people, I donate lots of money'. Actually those living styles or attitudes could simply create more desire and more anxiety for the people who work for them, or for the people who try to own those products.

I want to emphasise that right livelihood is to have a job which does not create more desire or anxiety in people. In any environment, if you have to fight, hurt people, harm others, discriminate against people, or judge them in order to get the job done, that is not suitable work. It will not provide a good working environment.

Defining the product of work

So what is work then? What is valuable work? What is harmful work? Work is *whatever we do*, whether it's at school as a student, or at home doing housework, in a paying job at the workplace, or even once we have retired or as a volunteer, say at a hospital, or at any non-profit organisation. All that is work. And whatever work draws you away from your centre, to possess, own, control, hurt or harm, it's not going to be the right job for you. What we all need is work that connects us with more people - more classmates, more friends, more colleagues - because that is going to help us be more humble, more selfless and more able to *let go* and this is the way we should learn.

Attitudes to work, and to others

We get so involved in working for work's sake, we forget that work is really another way for us to reach wisdom. It's not really some job that needs to be done, just as we clean the house and make sure nobody messes up. Actually, cleaning up is for people to mess up! That is not really a job at all. It's an act of love, an act of exchange. If we try to produce any product, it's because we need to share some kind of responsibility, and we want to exchange. I need some milk, so I produce vegetables, and I exchange them, and get milk. I produce car parts, and I get fruit, I produce toilet paper, whatever. It's because we want to contribute and share. But people who produce computers think 'computers are more important.' Or you produce vegetables 'Oh, vegetables are not important.' And because of that wrong attitude people become arrogant because they think 'I am more skilled' and so on. 'You are a farmer. You clean the street. Oh, you are not important.' That's not right. We have been brought up to place value on the wrong things. So those people think they are not doing an important job, and they feel inferior. They look down upon themselves, they feel depressed. And they try to change their work status and they think, 'Oh, after I get this job, I am going to be powerful, I'm going to be important. I'm going to be rich, I'm going to be successful, and I'm going to be happy!' Not necessarily. The President of the United States may not be happy. The rich billionaire may not be happy at all. That is not the answer.

Everybody has different needs. The boss is scared because without orders, and contracts, without business coming in, he will lose money. People have to control their desires. All of us have different ways to show our fear. But this world is balanced. If there is too much demand, there is less supply. So you can ask a higher price. So we have to balance the development of the community with the needs of individuals. As lots of people learn to work with computers, jobs in computers will become difficult to find. But not many people are studying to be farmers. So farmers will become very valuable. We need to balance our need and our greed or we will never have enough.

Moving away from a painful job

Some people think Buddhism says, "You're working in an unpleasant environment, these are challenges that come to you. Your karma has put you in that environment, so you can't just run away from it and expect it to go away. If you move away, at your next job you will meet with the same issues, because it's your karma." Another way to look at this is: "This unpleasant job is not right livelihood. I should actually choose to remove myself from this environment."

Growing gently into wisdom

Where is the karma? Karma is that you're not in control of the present situation. Basically none of us here on earth is in control. We are not free yet. So we are being controlled by the environment. But there are many choices we can make that help us move a little bit higher and become lighter every day. So we need to be protected by the environment, by the people, so we can move up to wisdom gradually. Not right away. Yes, one day you will feel you can work with these 'difficult' people. But not now. Right now, you will be affected by those negative behaviours, those thoughts, those defilements, you will not be able to let go and you will become influenced by them. You are not yet enlightened enough to deal with those behaviours. Before you are enlightened you need to be surrounded by a support group, because your real mind is always trying to heal itself, and needs a fairly calm space to do that work. The mind is just like a pool of dirty, muddy water. If you don't stir it, it will clear and become purified. So if we are easily irritated by the environment, it stirs up the mud in our minds. In a supportive environment, our irritation will clear. Just like a cloud that covers the moon, it will go away, the moon will be there without being hidden. Our minds are the same thing. That's why we need to go to the monastery to do meditation, or to church to pray, or to a quiet place in nature where we can be restored. In this way, we are protecting our real mind to get on with the job of healing itself.

Choosing a pleasant work place

When we are overwhelmed, we do not need to pick up more attachments, more defilements, more imprints, more and more. We will stop this real mind finishing its job if we overwhelm it. Most of our relationships should be calm and pleasant. So we need to be protected by about 80% of the people around us. We need to have supportive people around us most of the time. That leaves 20% of people who will warn us, 'Oh, I still have lots of ego. I still have lots of self to let go.' So this 20% of 'irritating' people are going to just warn us, awaken us to learn more about ourselves. But the 80% must be there to support us. Don't give yourself a hard time, don't give yourself more imprints to hold on to or attach to. We need to move on. If we are married to the right person, we will be protected by our spouse. At work, we may have good workplace companions. Maybe we belong to a church group, a temple group, some kind of volunteer group, where we can go and be with friends, so we are being protected by many, many different sources and environments. But there will be some small minority group that we cannot just go way from, that we have to deal with.

Once in a while we have to be there, no matter what. We have no choice. If you have a very strong support group in the office, and maybe just one tough guy to deal with, that's fine. But if 90% of work colleagues are hard to deal with, you'll have to go away. Leave. If you don't, you will be drawn in, you will sink into the depths, you will bury yourself. So you need to give yourself a break. Tell yourself, "I'll do it later, when I'm stronger, I'll come back. One day these people will support me, but not now. I am really dying. I cannot handle it. So I have to move on". Wait till you are wiser, like the Rinpoche, the wise sage, before going back to some terrible routine. The Rinpoche can cope with great pain and suffering. He has been practising for thousands of lifetimes. So he can do it. You think, 'He can do it, so I can do it.' You cannot. Because we need to have thousands of lives of sound introspective practice in the future to make it possible. So we have to find our own pace, our own schedule, and really find our own support groups to prepare ourselves, at our own speed, to become wise.

Your view, others' view

In our working environment, we suffer, torture ourselves and harm others. We think, 'The job should be done this way'. But we're only thinking, judging from our own point of view, looking at our own capabilities. Sometimes we hire someone, and over-estimate their capability, and they do less than we expected. Or we may misjudge them and expect them to do very badly, but they do very well. And then it becomes very messy, because we have not seen these people exactly as they are. So that's why, when we are working with people, we must realise that we don't yet really know what others are and what they want. We only know from our point of view: 'This is the way, this is the job'. So if you are a businessman, always thinking about 'This is the profession I have, I want to produce this kind of product only', you could have a very unsuccessful business. You should be thinking about what the *consumer* wants, what the *customer* wants, not what *I* want. Maybe you are good in this field, but your needs are *your* needs, not other people's needs, or other people's interests. Look beyond yourself. We think like this because we are so selfish. We have to be very careful.

The photographer's problem

Here is a fine example of the kind of issues we face at work that help us become wiser. A photographer told me this story:

"I have ten people working for me, and I try to run the business in a way that everyone has a say in the business, and people can grow in the business and develop themselves, but I still find we are in a situation where so much of our society is involved in creating desire. We don't need all the things that are in the supermarkets, but advertising makes everybody think we do need these things, even if we consider ourselves sophisticated and well-educated, we're still caught in the trap of wanting the nice car and the nice clothes. And other people with fewer things, fewer opportunities are even more caught in the trap.

"Our work is to take photographs, and sometimes the things we photograph are not good. We can see they're not well made. They are cheap and horrible. The manufacturers are offering credit to the buyers, so someone who can't afford this possession thinks that he *can* afford it. This poor man craves what he thinks is a good piece of furniture. He becomes almost like a slave working every month to pay for rubbish that's already broken before he's finished paying for it, that he didn't need to start with.

"Where my industry fits in is that, as photographers, we make this piece of badly built furniture look really, really good. You open the newspaper and look at the ad for it, and it looks fantastic. If we don't make it look good, the manufacturer won't pay us for the photographs. He says, "It looks like a piece of rubbish." Actually it *is* a piece of rubbish, but we disguise it through our photography, so the buyer will think he's getting a good deal. I have a problem with this. Because on the one side I think what we are doing in the company is good – we look after our staff well, we pay for people to go on treats and outings and training courses, but at the same time the company is doing this sort of work. It's a problem. It's not right speech. It's misrepresentation. Is it right livelihood? And it's not just us as photographers, it's people working for the banks, it's people that sell the stuff, the people that make the stuff. Everybody is caught in this trap."

What is the problem this photographer is experiencing? It is related to right speech. We have a very bad educational system, where teachers teach us to *pretend*. "Keep this inside of you. Don't tell everyone. Try to please everyone. Try to make everyone believe that you're so friendly and so gentle and so honest, even when you're not. This thing you want to talk about, don't dare tell people. Keep it quiet." When you were young, your parents were already telling you, "Just listen, and do what you're told. Don't argue with me. You're just a child." Then you go to school and the teacher and the other kids in the class teach us to hide things, not to speak out, to keep quiet. We do this so much, hiding what we feel, what we know is true, telling 'white' lies, that eventually, we don't even realise we are lying, we don't know we are cheating at all.

We have been programmed to think that this is the right way to behave, that this is right speech. So, whenever we feel something is wrong, and we speak out about it, we become a minority: people get angry, and reject us, and we become so isolated and so lonely. People feel we are too straightforward. They feel we are too honest. They feel we are out of control. We talk about the things that are really in our hearts, and let people know what is in our minds, and expose ourselves. So because we have been programmed to believe that true success is to be wanted and admired by others, and the most important thing in life is to own lots of things, we suppress our innate honesty, in order to be accepted.

Karma at work

Some Buddhists think, 'If I am sick, I have karma. If I lose my job, I have karma.' That's not right. That's not karma. Creating karma is the *action that you take* when you are in the job that you don't enjoy, that's karma, because you give up your control. You take actions and do things that you are not comfortable with. If you're sick but you can live with it, and if you are poor, and you can be with it, that's not karma. That's just the natural way things are, that's all. It's like one day it rains and another day it's sunny. Sunny day, windy day, it's just natural. If you are smart or you're dumb, sick, beautiful, ugly, whatever, it's the same. But if you're beautiful and are *proud and arrogant*, that will affect your karma, because it will affect the way you act. If you are rich, but *stingy and mean*, you are out of control and there is a karmic lesson for you there, because your attitude will affect your behaviour. But people don't understand. People go to school and to church and learn things, and also don't really understand what the teaching is about. The teaching is not for you to gloat over the fact that you have a good life, luck, merits – a good life is just another experience, that's all, just like an experience with poverty.

I had some people ask me about karma, related to someone who committed suicide. Suicide is not just jumping from a high-rise building, or hanging or shooting oneself. That is not the only way of committing suicide. Feeling depressed is also committing suicide. Feeling unwanted is also committing suicide. There are many ways to show that you want to end your life. To be violent is also committing suicide. People pretend it isn't. Drinking wine, smoking, is the same thing, we just give it a different name. People feel that having money is a better goal than being peaceful. But being peaceful is like having money. You feel in control. It's also richness. It's the same as riches in the pocket. You are an artist, and lead a wonderful life, but you are not wealthy, with lots of money. People are mistaken about the meaning of wealth. They think 'rich' must mean having lots of money, and if you don't have money, you're not rich. If you have to suffer at work for ten months to take a two months' retreat, that's not wealth. If you have to cheat customers and lie to them, you will need twenty years' retreat for those forty years of lousy work. But even twenty years to recover is not enough, because you have already programmed yourself to cheat yourself, because you cheat others. So, if you cheat yourself, and you try to wake up from this bad dream, sometimes it's not easy, because that behaviour is already imprinted on your mind. You never find anything to erase it, even attending a retreat.

The best practice

The best practice wherever you are, is to be honest, and not cheat others. If anyone pushes you to be dishonest, to harm, hurt, reject or discriminate against others, leave that kind of environment. Relieve yourself. There will be other wonderful people who are honest who will accept your kindness. You don't have to think 'I have to be here.' Just like when everyone goes drinking, and the bar is crowded with people, it's not the bar owner's problem. People want it. They go there by choice. They take in alcohol of their own free will. So you allow your boss to abuse you. You allow your colleagues to abuse you. You probably think that it's them abusing you. Oh, no, it's not. No. If you don't allow them to abuse you, they won't be monsters. Don't allow your clients to abuse you, by expecting you to be dishonest. There are other clients around. It may seem hard for the business, but it's the right thing for personal growth. Advertising does not have to be dishonest. Photography does not have to be dishonest. It can be true to reality and pure. No profession or work has to be dishonest.

Integrity at work

Sometimes we are confronted by one or two people in the workplace who trouble us. How can we get on better with the boss, who we do not like or trust, without losing our own integrity? In fact, how can we deal with a general lack of integrity at work?

Choose to work with colleagues who help you not only generate income but also allow you to be sincere, honest and satisfied with every action. You should not have to wait until the pay cheque or bonus or promotion has been given to feel satisfaction. To wait for the vacation is easy, if there's no need for escape. If you look forward to work every day, your relationships there are fine. If you have to go away on holiday to get rest and relief, you are really not happy with what you are doing now. If you have contact with others who give you peace of mind, and allow you to develop at your own pace, you will find the world beautiful. Surrounded by the opposite, you will find the world miserable. If you don't have a good family, good friends and good relationships with your colleagues at work, you will see the world as torturing.

Dealing with dishonesty

How do we deal with a dishonest person in a compassionate way, keeping our own principles firm, but not being horrible? How do we deal with the client who asks us to do things that involve lying and cheating? Actually you cannot be compassionate to the client if the client is not compassionate. Your message won't be received properly. He or she is not you. So you can only prepare yourself, prepare your words and your thoughts, and say what you want to say. Relax and feel comfortable when you are talking to the client. Whatever their reaction, you don't have control, you don't know what it will be. We can only feel comfortable if we let the client know that everybody has a different point of view. It may seem difficult. Maybe you are not satisfied with it, but this is normal.

Hurting yourself to help others?

We try to be successful in our businesses because we are thinking, 'I have ten people working for me and they are going to be protected by being in my business'. But if you have to hurt your conscience then you are not helping those colleagues either. So that means if you are balanced, the world is balanced. If you are balanced, you have a strong positive energy. So you don't have to do anything to show your goodness, to show your contribution to the world, and to the people. If you have lots of money you don't need to give it to the church or the temple. If you pay your bills on time, pay your suppliers on time, pay your employees, if you appreciate others, allow people to make some profit out of your business, things like that, that is charity. That is also a donation, a contribution. If you have the benefit of others in your thoughts and in your mind always, you will be running a good business.

People think, 'I need a big business to raise my kids, I need a bigger business to do charity work, I need this huge business to help my colleagues make lots of money', it puts too much pressure on you. There are many ways to help. You don't need to run a business thinking 'I have to sacrifice my integrity for other people's interests.' If we all think this way, believing we are licensed to act badly, that it's OK to be dishonest, we are doing ourselves real harm. *It's OK to be honest.* We all have to allow people to make some reasonable profit. Because we exchange. We need to make a fair exchange. What is a fair salary for a gardener? What is a fair salary for a programmer? There are no standards at all. More demand creates more supply. So if someone finds there is a great demand for her product or service, she may say, 'Ten thousand dollars is my price." I deliver my order, I make it easy for you and easy for myself. Lots of people produce very good products. They ask high prices, and why not? It's OK. There is nothing wrong with earning a good living. But you cannot pretend you have a good product and ask an expensive price if it's a lie.

Support for artists

As a photographer you are an artist. We should support artists, because artists help pass on human culture to the next generation. We need to help those who have beauty in their hearts and minds so they are able earn a good living. Time is important for them. They need to have precious time to be creative, and to beautify the world and beautify people's minds, with precious artwork. So I think it's quite important that we should be well off, we should be successful, but we must more than anything be comfortable with the work we do.

Different standards, different prices

We have many different standards, not only one standard. If you see this picture is marvellous, you will pay R10 000 for it. But maybe the artist only wants to be paid R1 000. I see the value as R10 000, because I want to support this artist to have more time to be creative, to create more good, so just for myself whenever I go out I feel I want to give. If I have to meet with someone in the coffee shop I want to give a large tip to the waitress. I just want to share how wonderful it feels if people are generous. I want to be a role model. They have to learn that giving is wonderful because it makes people happy, and when others are happy, you are happy. So if you come to the temple to work I will ask you how much money you need. So you say, "I need R10 000. It's what I need." But another time, you may want only R1 000 because you don't need so much money. Not everyone needs to get R10 000. Maybe some people are rich, and they don't want any money, they want to give more. But some have family, or have children, they want to raise their children and have some kind of a savings fund for their children's education. There's not only one standard. There are many different points of view, different needs, and different standards.

Different salaries

Sometimes we feel we are underpaid for the work we do, and this makes us resentful. What should I do if I think I am poorly paid? How can I get more money? This is a difficult question. In this world, never look for justice. Never ask, "Why?" Never expect to know the reason for everything. Life is complicated. There are so many causes and conditions that affect the circumstances of our lives. While everybody needs money, what is enough? Sadly, it will probably never be enough, if all you are working for is the money. The best philosophy is that saving is earning. If you can try to save some of your income, you have already earned more.

If you are not satisfied with what you've been paid, you need to consider whether you can easily be replaced. Yes, you can leave your job. But will you find better pay elsewhere? If you can get better pay somewhere else, then why stay? In this world, business works on the supply and demand principle. If you have qualifications that nobody else has, you can ask whatever price you like for your services. But people will pay you less if there are too many people with your level of skill. Then no matter how hard you ask for more money, you will only have more frustration. This is the human tragedy, the human crisis.

We live in fear, worrying about the future. We save because we are certain that in future we will not have enough. So if you have that state of mind, saving makes you feel poor. You think, 'It will get worse tomorrow. Next year will be even worse.' Asking for more never ends, because of our cravings, and cravings are never satisfied.

As an employer, if you allow a staff member to select his own salary he will never ask for less. The war to acquire wealth and possessions is never ended. Even entrepreneurs and business owners have worries, take risks and incur debts, while they make and lose money. The main thing to remember is that no one will stay rich or poor all the time. Our fortunes are always changing. Here is an example. Imagine a student in the USA who has $5000 in his pocket and two suitcases. Twenty years later, he has one wife, two daughters, a job, a house, a car, a degree, a home and $200 000 debt. Is he rich or is he poor compared to twenty years before? He has debts and mortgages, responsibilities, commitments now that he didn't have then. In understanding changing fortunes, and the coming and going of wealth, the only protection is being in control of the mind.

Teamwork

At work, we grow through our relationships with others. In order to grow, we need to work together. We need to start thinking, 'This is *our* company, not *my* company; *our* product or service not *mine*.' We all need to realise that we are only part of the business. Without a group of people to work together, the firm would not exist. If you are running your own company, you may be aware that the staff do not understand you, they do not perform as well as you do. Well, that's why they're not the MD or CEO. You contribute what you can, and they do the same. But it's the output from all the employees together that delivers the goods. You are not so important. They are not so little. It's not *your* target, it's *our* target. We have to work together to make it happen. You may contribute more because you have more wisdom and power. You may lead lazy, confused, selfish people or you may lead mature people. Everybody has a different state of mind, a different level of awareness. But don't make the mistake of thinking that you're managing them, controlling their performance, you're not really. They contribute what they are willing to give, and that's all.

Think of it this way: You have to allow all the staff to contribute according to their own ability to serve. So everyone shares the responsibility. They create problems, you solve them. Don't try to avoid problems. As the boss, it's your job and your honour to sort things out. You are there for your staff whenever they need you. If there are no problems, the workers won't need a manager. So you need to allow people the possibility of failure, and be there to help solve the problems, not punish or judge or blame. The manager is like a shoulder to them, a shoulder to lean on, a shoulder to cry on. You are a servant of the work community, and in being that you are successful, wise and powerful. So much so that they want to rely on you when they need you. If there are no workers, you cannot be the manager. They allow you to become the manager.

From the worker's point of view

Not all of us are managers or owners of businesses. As workers, we can easily become jealous. Why don't I get a promotion? Why no bonus? Why do I have to do this tedious work? We are not humble. We don't do our work properly. We duck out, we avoid responsibility, or we try to do things we're not qualified for. We will have enemies. At work there will be some who recognise us, and some who bully us. At any level, we need to work towards having a balanced mind. Some colleagues will support you. Others won't. Accept those people who abuse you. Nobody can tell you the way out of bad relationships. If you have a good group of people at work who accept you, you tend to hide your negative defilements. You don't have the same pressure to be pleasant at home, so those defilements come up. You are continually faced with your state of mind when you work with people. That's why there are so many years of preparation with family and friends, to help us when we encounter those toughest relationships of the world of work.

How can I make friends at work?

If you have humility in you, you will see, 'This colleague will teach me something'. If you are willing to be instructed, and respect your colleagues, it will be easier for them to open up, so you can build a relationship with them. Without that humbleness and openness to learning, it's difficult. Openness will motivate you to help your colleague – it will help you realise, 'He's a great manager, I want to help him!' You work to let go of your ego, your ambition to push yourself past others. Work to help the manager, the seniors, and this respect and interest will help you to build better relationships with your colleagues.

The relationship with the actual job

Sometimes we work with great people, but the actual work we do is not fulfilling. We have great fun relating to our work colleagues, but doing the job itself fills us with dismay. It's never too late to make another plan. You will become more and more unhappy if you don't start working towards making a change, and finding another kind of work. There is more to life than this particular type of work. Through your work you connect with the whole world and with people. If you end your life filled with hatred for your work, you will enter another life taking that hatred with you. You will draw those feelings along with you. By changing your job you may need to get a smaller house, and give up some of your material possessions. What you have is not making you happy. Possessions do not make you happy.

Bosses who ask too much

Some people feel they are always being asked to do more work, without being paid more. It makes them angry. What can they do?

If you are anxious about 'being made to do more' in the same hours at work, it means you haven't let go of the work you have already completed. Any new work feels like an extra burden. So the pattern of work should be: 'Do it. Let go. Do it. Let go.' with each task or project. You will have energy for more activity that way. For those people who feel tired by the demands made by the boss, try this technique. You are also tired because you don't enjoy what you are doing. In Egypt they built pyramids without machinery. Now people use machinery, but people still get tired at work. Why? It's not because the work takes too much physical energy. It's because people don't have a 'relaxed mind.' Their busy, confused thoughts take so much energy away from their bodies.

If you are unhappy in your work, it may be that you are thinking too much. You are comparing. You are jealous. You are arguing. That makes you very tired all the time. If you enjoy what you are doing, it won't bother you. You will get to the end of the day at work and feel as fresh as the morning, if you love your work and do it honestly. If you hold negative emotions, it takes away your energy and exhausts you. If the job is done, what is the extra time for? To do more work, with happiness. Just enjoy your work and make each day a full one.

This does not apply when your boss is extending your working hours beyond what is reasonable, and making you work overtime and weekends without pay. But generally, most hurt is from ourselves. If a demand upsets you, think about negotiating with the person making that demand. Let your boss understand your limitations. Sometimes that feeling you are getting is not from your boss; it's from within you. You control yourself. Why be irritated by one demand? That 'noise' is from your inside. You are not able to let your emotion out. Let your boss know how you feel. Don't let that one sentence bother you for many years. Only those people who are not balanced can easily be affected by a single person or a single instruction. You may have unpleasant contacts with people, but if you have calm and energy within, you let go the unpleasant. You might have a bad boss, but your relationship with the company, the suppliers and the customers will energise you to deal with your impossible boss (or your ego). In one day you have many encounters. You have contact with the trees, the sky, and at once you are already away from that previous unpleasant contact. One contact should not be irritating if you know how to balance your mind by bringing your attention to the present, and letting go of the past.

Work and other relationships

I love my work but it has taken over my life, and I have no outside interests. All my other relationships are dying. What should I do?

Any job is always related to people. If you can't relate to people you have the wrong attitude. Your work really becomes valuable when you let the people around you energise your heart. That means helping the people who need your services. Say you are doing landscaping, or cleaning, or making perfumes, or selling fruit and vegetables, or working for the government - it's the people who use your service or product that you do it for. You work for the customers, the end users, not only for your boss. Work should not separate you from your relationships, it should help you build more of them.

Some people use work to escape from relationships. They see work as something separate from relationships. They don't see 'the many in one'. If you are not open-minded, you will only see the work itself, and forget that you are actually supported by many relationships and many people while you work. You are not separate from relationships. You cannot survive to live alone. And your job can never be done only by you. You need to be humble and realise non-self. You are part of others, and they are part of you. You are one in many and many in one.

What is 'one in many and many in one'?

If we stop and think, we will see that our bodies, our cells, are made up of elements that are from outside. We breathe in air and eat food, so our bodies absorb those 'non-me' things and they become 'me'. Likewise we feel other people's emotions, their suffering, their joy, and it becomes part of us. We share our thoughts and wishes and time with others, and they absorb some of us into themselves. So we intermingle, we move into inter-being. This is the many-in-one and the one-in-many. The more we realise that we are part of a greater whole, the less lonely and cut off we feel, and the happier we are. We also become more aware that our actions can hurt or harm others, and caring about them, we think before we act. This more kindly way of living - being aware of our links with others, our inter-being with others - brings us more peace.

Someone to love

Someone to Love

All of us long to be free from emotional pain and suffering. As human beings we struggle very hard to understand life and our role and purpose in it. How then do we liberate ourselves, and reach peace? We do it through love. We start by loving our parents, our brothers and sisters. Later, we learn through loving our husband or wife and children. Wherever love is, love helps us to be free, because instead of feeling separate from other beings, love helps us to realise that we are not alone. This is a major step towards enlightenment.

The best start to a relationship

How do I prepare myself for a meaningful sexual or marital relationship? Well, we have many years to prepare. We have around twenty years with family and friends, teachers, classmates, and people with whom we share common interests. This gives us a very good foundation to learn about building relationships. As we grow up, we build skills that allow us to relate to others. We start to realise what is important to us, and what to look for when we choose a life-partner who will help us live in peace and grow in wisdom.

Your examples of love

Loving others is not always easy. The first family may have taught you unhealthy ways of relating to others. Your first family may have been strained and unhappy. In childhood, possibly you didn't get along with your brothers or sisters. Maybe you didn't get along with your parents. You may now avoid being with them. These unhappy first family relationships do not make it easier to love a life partner, because your role models did not provide you with the best skills.

On the other hand, you may have become dependent on your first family. Instead of dislike, you feel a desperate need to be with them. The family may hold together so strongly that others are excluded. You may have become so attached to your first family, you are scared to let go. Sometimes you have a deep need to stay with your parents. You have to be with them and no one else, you are so afraid to lose them. You turn love into fear, or doubt or jealousy. You have this craving to be only with your first family, you are unwilling to move away and grow up. These patterns make finding a life partner more difficult.

Wanting to be loved

As you reach adulthood, you feel the need to create your own loving relationship. If you have had a disturbed first family, you think, 'This time, I'm going to do it right. This will be *my* choice.' As a young adult, you think, 'I'm going to find someone to love and *I* will be responsible. I will choose someone who is perfect for me. There will be no problems, no hassles, no quarrels.' You think, 'I have had this relationship with my family for so many years now, it's time for me to grow up, leave the family, and make my own life. I want to be with someone who will love me for what I am.' In adulthood, you do your best to find someone you feel you can love deeply in order to become fulfilled. The sad thing is that many of us go into adult relationships not really looking for someone to love, but for someone to *love us*. We ask ourselves, "How much does he love me?" We may not admit it, but we may be feeling, 'I love him because I want him to love me back.' We think, 'I love you – you must love me!' We start to date someone and dream that this person must be Mr or Ms Right – and if not, we are going to change them! We consider a relationship from the point of view of our own benefit. This is not unconditional love. It's very conditional, and will not really bring us happiness.

It is a paradox. Most young adults want to be separate from their families. They long for their independence, they think that adulthood is all about standing on their own two feet, running their own life, leaving others behind, being alone. But real independence comes through realising we are not separate from others. Choosing a loved one, learning to understand a hated one, that is our mission in this world, and it will take us many lifetimes of learning about love and hate before we become liberated.

Fear and clinging

We all know how romantic falling in love can be. At the start of a new romance, you feel you have lots to share with each other. You have such fun being together, you have so much to talk about. You enjoy loving each other, and nothing else seems to matter. So you start to think about commitment. You want to be married. But at the same time you are frightened. Possibly, you start to feel you want more control, because this is a life-long commitment. 'I must keep this relationship forever because I love him, and I must have him love me for the rest of this life.' Afraid of losing the other, we cling more tightly.

The same or different?

At the start of a relationship, we don't realise that we are different from our partners, in that we have had different past experiences, a different upbringing and maybe even different cultural values. As a result, we may see things from different points of view. Your loved one behaves differently to what you expect. She seems like a stranger. You cannot make your spouse behave the way you expect him or her to. It's a great shock.

What happens when we feel this fear? When suddenly the feeling of being in love wears off a little, and we see the other person as having their own will and their own identity, and not wanting what we want at all? We try to control them. Because we cannot control our parents, or our brothers and sisters, we think we can control this life partner, this husband or wife. We think, 'Because I am an adult, very smart, very wise now, I know what I want. I can run my own life, and do what I like. I am in charge.' We forget that we are only in charge of ourselves. Realising that we have a lot to learn about our partners, and that they have the right to think and act in a way that is right for them, is often a difficult lesson.

My partner is me

Our life partners may seem like strangers to us, because we have not listened and looked deeply and learned about them. Our partners are not just strangers. In fact, they are also very, very familiar. Because the partner I choose is really myself. Like attracts like. We choose 'ourselves'. Our partners are our projections of ourselves.

There is a story about a firm that was relocating from Johannesburg to Cape Town. One of the staff asked a wise person about the new city. "What are the people like in Cape Town?" The wise person said, "Well what are people like in Johannesburg?" "They are hard-working, straight talking, and friendly." "You will find them the same in Cape Town," the wise person replied.

Another employee also wanted to know about people in Cape Town. The wise person asked her, "How do you find people in Johannesburg?" and she replied, "They are bullies, rude and greedy." "You will find the Cape Town people are just the same," said the sage.

This is an old story. You have probably heard it told about another country or another time. The truth it illustrates is that we see ourselves reflected in the people around us. We are the companions we choose.

In the same way, the life partners we choose reflect qualities we have in ourselves. Not everyone realises this. People sometimes wonder, 'If I'm going to choose a life-partner, how do I make sure he's good or bad?' The truth is, he or she will be like you. We choose ourselves. If you haven't been purified and let go of attachments in twenty years, and become beautiful inside, you're going to choose a painful person. Because you yourself are a painful person. Because you are also suffering. What you are is what your partner is. Because your actions bring out good or bad in her, your partner will reflect you. If you are up on the mountain you will have a clear view, but if you're at the bottom of the valley, then you won't have a clear view. It's just the same in choosing a mate. If a person's mind is clouded, and filled with cravings and obsessions, hatred and greed, he or she will choose someone who is familiar with those feelings as well. This is the kind of person he will be comfortable with. They will share the same problems and needs and views of life.

A difficult but worthwhile way of learning about ourselves is to closely study our partners. We will see ourselves reflected there, and will learn things (some unpleasant, some painful) about how we are. This is uncomfortable, but it gives us a way of rebuilding our relationship through changing our own dark sides. Because when we let go of those patterns in ourselves, our partner will no longer dramatise them. We will no longer be feeding that habit or pattern of thinking in him or her, so it will tend to diminish and even disappear.

Sharing ourselves, learning about each other

Not many of us really understand ourselves completely - we are so confused and lost, we don't know who we are or what we want. How then can we possibly understand someone else? With this false idea in our minds, we judge our life partner, and have expectations. 'If he does this, if she doesn't do that, then I will be happy.' The truth is that even if your partner behaves in the way you insist on, you may still be unhappy, because you may not really know what you want either. So because we have lost ourselves and each other, thinking we are now what we were in the past, our relationship starts to grow cold. We become more and more lonely and alienated. We are afraid to talk about it, and we hide this sadness away, though we long for our relationship to be restored.

The myth we carry into marriage

How do we move from this pain to a new level of understanding? First we need to get rid of the idea that we can change someone else. Of course, you can share whatever you think about who he is or what he needs, but he is himself, he has his own mission to improve himself, you can't do it for him. You can't do it for her. Even though I think I have a better way of living, a better attitude, I still cannot just convert my loved one to be the person I think they should be. We think, 'She's an alcoholic. But I'll reform her. I'll change her. My love will change her.' Or we think to ourselves, 'He's a money-grabbing miser. He's mean. But I will change him.' This is one of the myths that we carry when we enter into marriage, hoping to change or reform our loved one.

This desire to change the other also moves people away from insight. They are left feeling irritated, cheated or betrayed. In truth, nobody betrayed them but their own false perceptions. They didn't know this other person at all. They judged rather than investigated, and then imagined they got a bad deal, when instead they had foolish expectations to start with. People start to argue and fight with their partners, and become bitter, because they miss this point. Expectations are not the same as reality. Our loved ones are the way they are, not the way we demand that they be. When we realise this, we can start to rebuild our relationships, by finding out who our partners really are, and what they really need from us.

We need the other person in order to become complete, because the other helps us to give, and to love, and to grow. Through our loved one, we learn to be connected, not to be separate from people. Having our partner there helps us do the work to become complete as a person.

Learning about ourselves

Deep within us, we have clarity. Deep in our consciousness we have wholesomeness, but we often ignore our deeper self. We act in ways that are not skilful, and by doing so, we block our wholesomeness.

Our deep inner self is always trying to help us reach understanding. But our powerful ego-driven urges ignore the wholesome reality. We may not be aware of it, but our deep inner self, our real mind is always trying to rescue us. So whenever we do something which goes against the real mind, this real mind sends out the message, "That's wrong, that's the opposite of what you should be doing, that's negative." We deeply recognise this. So we feel broken, because of the hatred we feel, because of the way we reject others, because of the irritation we feel, the hurt we cause, the pain we make others suffer. Only when we really let go of these unwholesome urges that come from the ego, will we suddenly feel that comfort, appeasement, and harmony within us. We are naturally whole, but the ego gives us this feeling of being separate and fragmented. Yes. So only when we let go of this ego, will we be able to hear the messages that our real mind is sending, of how to heal ourselves, cure ourselves and bring ourselves back home to the centre of our being.

What is ego?

Ego is simply our thoughts, emotions and behaviour patterns, linked to the past, that we think make us different and alone and separate from others. Your ego kicks in when you don't live your life one moment at a time. There's a shadow in you, and this shadow tells people "I'm forty years old. I'm Mr Smith. I am a professor." That is ego. But if you only live in this moment, you don't need that identification with labels. You are only here at this moment. You are not re-born, you are *new-born* every moment. Always here. Always one moment. You die again. And you are reborn in the next moment, with no shadow from the past. If you carry that shadow, that ego, you are going to block out a portion of reality, and you are broken, because you are not here, totally 100%. Ego prevents us from living in the present. You have certain habits in dealing with people, a certain way of dealing with friends, you have preferences about food, preferences of being with certain people. This is the conditioned part of your mind controlling you. In your past world, your present world, your future world, you have your family, you have strangers, you have loved ones, hated ones. You judge the present based on your past experiences, based on old, worn-out concepts that may no longer apply. Because of ego, you do not see things freshly, as they really are, this instant.

So we have this ego. But the real self is trying to get rid of these old patterns, these worn-out concepts, trying very hard. So whenever this ego is acting up, your real self is going to make you unsettled and uncomfortable, encouraging you to examine yourself and find out what is out of balance.

For many people, appearances are everything. People *are* their conditioning. I am a man, a woman, South African, English, Zulu. That's all they know about who they are. They don't know there is a deeper part within them, which is the real self. So that's why people blame other people or material things, or events for their own unhappiness. "Oh, it's you who are making me miserable." or "Lack of money is taking away my joy and happiness." They are not realising the reality. By focussing on the money, they are missing the reason for life.

The obsession with money cuts you off from everything else. The same thing happens when you think only about your husband or your wife, you cut yourself off from everyone else, so you risk losing everyone else, and your real mind feels the loss, and you feel broken.

The truth is, we are happiest when we connect with others. The more connections we have, the happier we are, because our deep inner self wants to be connected to the whole universe. But because of that ego attachment, that clinging, those ego memories of unhappy past experiences where you felt rejected, unloved and disconnected, you mistakenly believe you only have your husband, you only have your wife. You don't realise you still have this tree, this flower, these friends, this beautiful sunset, these laughing children. You think you don't have these connections. So you get scared, without really knowing why. You think maybe it's because you could lose your husband or wife, but actually it's not that. It's because you see your husband or wife as the only person you can love and be connected with. You don't see friends, you don't see strangers as connected to you. You don't get in touch with your brothers and sisters any more. So the pain that you feel is the message the real mind is sending out. Your deepest self is sending a warning. You feel broken whenever you attach yourself to someone whether through hate or through love. Your real mind, your deepest self tries to rescue you, and help you let go of this attachment that blinds you to the love that surrounds you from every point in the universe.

How can one get rid of all these attachments and conditions and get through to one's real mind? In fact, paradoxically, attachments will help us to get rid of attachments. Our relationship with our marriage partner or significant other is helping us to become free.

Growing from attachment to freedom

We start learning from the one attachment that is going to help us get rid of ego more easily. For example you love your wife. And because you love your wife, you forget about what you want, and instead you give your wife whatever she wants. Because you have a strong attachment to her, you love her, you long for her, you want to please her, and hold her close to you, you easily empty out these selfish feelings that 'This is my tea, this is my bed, this is my house, this is my money, this is my hobby.' Instead, you ask her, "What do you want, what kind of food do you want to try, where do you want to travel?" In doing this, in trying your best to please your loved one, you are learning how to be selfless. And selflessness brings peace, calm and wisdom.

Because we tend to do things from a selfish point of view, we have to reverse this selfishness in order to find true happiness. We have to wash our selfishness away. By pleasing and caring for the other person, we learn to be selfless. This is how the habit of loving someone helps us release the suffering caused by ego. Maybe we have been saying, "This is what I want. Join me. I want Chinese food. I don't want Italian." We should listen to ourselves. Instead of saying, "Listen to me. This is my will. This is my wish. This is my plan." We could choose to say, "OK, your choice is my choice." This is the way you learn to let go of this shadow, this ego. It may appear that we get into a love relationship out of selfishness, because it feels good, but even though it may be motivated by selfishness, with practice it can turn into altruism. In your deepest heart, you love the trees, you love the flowers, you love nature, you love your brother and sister, but you need to find someone or something to help you get started on this loving, to help you develop this habit of caring about others, this habit that will ultimately lead to freedom.

When are we ready for marriage?

We need to prepare, to practice for a long life together. We have ten, twenty, thirty, forty years to prepare. Everyone needs a different length of time to get ready, to be committed to a long-term relationship. Some people are very childish. Many people, when they get married, are not really ready. They have to be responsible for this choice and this person, and be able to work it out with the other. But some people need many more years to prepare themselves. Just because you are an adult and have a job doesn't mean you're ready for marriage or a committed relationship. Having a job, money, a house or a car is not enough. It's not like that.

Can you wait too long before getting married and settling down? No not really. A person who is ready will not feel the need to wait. If you're ready, you will have a kind of joy at the thought of being committed. That means that for those people who are reluctant to be committed, there's a reason. It's because they're not ready. Only people who are ready will feel that longing to be joined to another, because it's so complete, so full, so rich. Nobody who is ready for commitment would want to lose this precious opportunity to be close to someone.

Sexual attraction as a reason for a relationship

What about sexual attraction, that drives people to get into relationships before they are ready for the commitment? Ah, Sex. Sex is not marriage. Sex is not having children. You can't say, "Because I'm having sex I'm going to be a good mother, and should have children." No, that's not healthy. Let's be honest about sex. You know that feeling you get when you crave sex. It's not much different from the craving you get for cigarettes, or alcohol, or food, or sweets, or excitement. Sex is basically a craving. People who are very sick, very congested, need lots of sex. If you are very healthy, you don't need so much sex at all. Sex is also a way of running away from problems. It's an escape. Indulging in massive amounts of sex just delays the purification of the body. It's like getting drunk. When you get drunk, you feel 'Oh, nothing is a problem.' It's a way to numb yourself. You choose alcohol or sex or drugs as a way to escape from the problems and the issues confronting you. Sadly, the problems and issues are still there after the hangover or the pregnancy or the HIV infection. Sooner or later, you will need to come back again to fix the problems.

When your body is congested, your body tries to heal itself, and to eliminate the poison, and you need energy to do this work of cleansing the body. When you have sex, you delay this process. It's wasted energy. Sex without love is a way of delaying problems that will have to be dealt with later. Eventually you have to come back to confront the problems. Eventually you will have to find the energy to cleanse the body. People who are craving sex are suffering from congested bodies, but they do not have enough energy to start the process of healing. At that moment they are partially dead. When you crave sex, you are not fully alive. So partially dead, it makes you feel good. You don't have to do the work to cleanse your body, and your body is not allowed to heal. So at that point of time, it's just as if you are entering into a kind of a coma. Sex is like drugs. Yes, it's an opiate, an escape.

Sex can be magnificent if you are already healthy, and love someone dearly, who you want to raise children with. You want to pass on your love to another loved one. The most tender, precious sex is that union to conceive a child. Only more aware people can enter into that kind of unification during sex. Sex may be a way of gaining enlightenment, but it is not the only way to enlightenment. Those higher beings that are enlightened don't need that kind of sex to become unified with the universe. People also say that about drugs. "You take LSD, you will be at one with the universe, you will understand Nirvana – it's just by taking something like cocaine that you find enlightenment." This is a dangerous concept and a false one.

Let me give you an example. If I have a headache now – I will stop my headache by drinking a sugary, caffeine-loaded cold drink. This drink is so poisonous to my system, it's going to take all my energy to get rid of the poison in the drink. So my body will put its attention on the elimination of the poison, and for a short time it will seem as if the headache has gone away. But it will create more problems for the future because if I delay cleansing my stomach – because a headache is often caused by the stomach – if I drink that cold drink, my body will use what energy it has to deal with the caffeine, and there will be no energy left to heal my body of the original poison that my stomach needs to clear. You delay your healing in this way for 10 or 20 years and then you will be incurable. So having repeated sex without love is like that. It can only harm you and your body.

If unloving sex is harmful, is celibacy good?

Yes, celibacy can be good, but not if it can only be done by exerting great control. If you desire sex, but force yourself to be celibate, that is not recommended. The proper natural way is to look after your body (see chapter 7), and allow it to heal. Look after your spiritual growth, and grow in wisdom. One day after you have a clean body, and an open, balanced mind, then you will find you no longer crave sex. You don't have to push yourself. There's no pressure or discipline. It's a slow process, and you go at your own speed.

As an example, whenever you feel, 'Oh, I'm so down, let me have some sugar.' That's OK. Because when you're so down, you need all your energy to get rid of that symptom of the illness. The sugar will stop the process of cleansing for some time, because you don't have the energy to do that much work. So this sugar will help you have a break. And you can say to yourself, "After I'm stronger, I'll do this work of cleansing." Sex is like that as well. "Let me just have some sex now, and I'll feel better, and I'll deal with the problems in my life then. Then tomorrow I'll handle my life. Right now, let me have some sex." That's what people do. It's a comfort. It's OK. But you need to know that this is not the answer to happiness. You know it's only for temporary relief. One day you will no longer crave sex, and that will happen when your body and mind are balanced.

Sexual relationships before marriage

When we know who we are, when we are balanced, we are able to support and comfort other beings, and have a good marriage. We don't encourage people to have sexual relationships first, before they are married. If the only reason you want a relationship is for sex, then this attitude is already giving you a signal that you're not yet ready for a meaningful relationship. You're not ready for the commitment that marriage requires. Although we may not yet be a hundred percent perfect, we still need a greater portion of the mind balanced and in control to form a good marriage. If you cannot control your desires to begin with before marriage, it will be easy for you to have the same problem during the marriage, for example by having love affairs with other people outside of your marriage, and that will cause the marriage some distress.

We all experience challenge during certain kinds of fasting periods – are you ready or not? How good is your control? It's like having a meeting in the bar. You can do that if you have control over your alcohol consumption. Then you are welcome to go to the bar for a meeting, because you won't be addicted to the liquor. If you are in control, you are allowed to be with a beautiful lady alone in a room, because you are not going to seduce or rape her. If before marriage you don't have any commitment and you have sex easily, you will almost certainly do the same thing afterwards, and in turn ruin your marriage.

We need to find the right kind of people before we make the decision to get married. If you want to fool around with promiscuous people, then don't talk about marriage. You only have sex with them. That's your choice. But not marriage. Because when you make a lifetime commitment, you aim for a different kind of person. I think sex is the last consideration when you are thinking about marriage. Just having sex with someone doesn't make you love them.

Sex is a way for a couple to relieve themselves of certain kinds of physical discomfort, like a very demanding itch that must be scratched. That is why you want someone who cares about you, who you love deeply, to give you this kind of support, to bring you this kind of relief from the physical burden. You have someone who loves you to help you to do this. So this is one way to show you love someone. But there are many other ways to show you love someone. It doesn't mean you only have sex with this person, if you are his wife or her husband. You do many other loving, caring things for them.

Some people talk about unwanted sex. Yes, in a marriage partnership there is so much we have to work together on. It's the food we eat, the life we live. If you eat more junk food, your body is more congested. So clearly, those sick people living on junk food are going to ask for more sex. Those stressful minds will ask for more sex. Those depressed minds will need more sex. So physically and mentally we need to be balanced. We need to talk it out, share and be honest and accept and be supportive, about what we each need. A higher state of mind brings less need for sex. But if there is an imbalance between partners, you will need to talk it through, and see if you can find solutions.

We change, loved ones change

Sometimes, we go into a relationship thinking our partner's commitment will be life-long. They are so devoted to us, they love us so deeply. Being aware that we are loved so strongly, we become absent-minded and careless about the relationship. We take their love for granted. We assume that they will love us forever and that nothing will change. This is also a big mistake.

The truth is that we change every day. Think about it. We are often not aware that all around us the world is changing. People around us change, and we have to be alive every moment to realise this. We need to be thinking, 'This partner of mine has changed. I must also have changed. How are we going to get together, make contact with each other, these new selves that we are?' We should ask ourselves this, but all too often we don't. How often do we bother to look at our spouse and ask him or her, "Who are you now? What matters to you right now? What's important in your life today?" We don't bother to do that. We think, 'Oh, we're married, and that's it! He will always be my husband. She will always be my wife. Everything is fine.' This way of thinking, assuming, 'Oh, I know who she is, I know who he is,' is a remnant of the past, because once in the past we thought we knew each other very well. Now, after living with this person for the past ten years, we may start to feel irritated, because they no longer fit in our lives as comfortably as they did before.

We are all growing - growing better, growing worse, we don't know - but we are all in the process of change. If we are judged or labelled according to how we used to be, or how someone else thinks we are, then we can feel frustrated, upset or angry. Try not to do this to your partner.

Losing touch with the other

What happens when you find you are married to someone you have nothing in common with? You seem to have lost touch completely. You are emotionally estranged from each other. You find you are angry or bitter in your relationship. If you find yourself with a very hot temper, it is because you don't know how to express yourself, or talk about what you have been feeling inside. You always hide it, and suppress it until one day it explodes. When you wake up one day and realise, 'He's so strange, he's so different', it's because you didn't do the work. Gradually, every day, every moment, you need to work on your relationship. You have to work problems out, to know each other better. Don't pretend. Don't hide the feeling. There is no point in thinking, 'This should be the way', and then not explaining your views to your partner, relying instead on your expectations and projections that things will come right by themselves. You are setting yourself up for a surprise in the future. Ten years from now. Boom! You'll get the big explosion.

So I always say that if you express your feelings every day, then there will be no war, because you won't have to fight. You *should* express your emotions. Every day. Every day, communicate - share your ideas and talk about your concerns. Then you don't have to start your cold war, or your quarrels or fights or separations. The separation comes because we didn't see each other freshly, and teach our loved one about ourselves freshly. We forgot that we are fresh and new every day. So we need to share, every day, to wake our partner up, and let them know, "The reality inside me is not what you think."

Extra-marital sex

Sadly, we may not have done this work. We may have become estranged. We may have needs we have not been able to share. If you are married to someone, and you have to find some other person to have sex with, then you must have a problem with your relationship because it is part of your loved one's duty to help you find a way to balance your body and your mind. You need to meet each other's sexual and emotional needs. In an extra-marital relationship you run the risk of getting yourself or your partner pregnant, and can easily create babies. So you need to be responsible for bringing another life into this world. If you are having sex with this person illegally, at that time your mind will be disturbed. You will be frightened, scared, feeling guilty, and this will invite a lower being to be conceived in this kind of sexual relationship. It's not the right environment for a new being to be brought into this world.

If you are not legally allowed to be with someone, you have to hide somewhere and meet in secret. You are going to be very nervous. You will pretend you are not Mr Smith or Mr Mokoena. You will use a different name to check into a hotel to do these different things. Or you will hide in the car, or do something in the dark. And that state of mind is not relaxing, it's tense, frightened, upset. Once you have started this kind of action, you tend to do more and more, until one day you are no longer comfortable with your loved one. Your mind will be filled with unwanted emotions, unwanted feelings, and those bad cover-ups. So you will feel guilty when you are with your wife or your husband, and this will cause you to cheat more, and tell more lies. An extra-marital sexual relationship will eventually cause you to separate from your loved one. Your loved one may not know, but your real mind knows, your deep inner self knows.

In some societies there is no pressure to be faithful. In others there is great pressure to be faithful. But the pressure or lack of pressure from others is not what is important. It must be you who wants to be faithful. Otherwise you will humiliate yourself with lots of lies, lots of cheating, and you will hate yourself in the end. Because if you betray your husband or wife, then as a natural consequence you will force yourself into lots of pretending, and this will not invite good energy from your spouse. Your spouse may not know about the affair, but the bad energy will be there between you. Eventually, you will drive him or her away.

Without making any moral judgement on the issues, eventually a couple where one is having sex outside of the marriage is going to break apart. That is because the one having sex outside doesn't deserve this marriage anymore. It's not punishment from God or from Buddha, or punishment from the group, it's punishment from him or herself, from his or her real mind. A person who has affairs while being married will feel so guilty and shameful. He may not be aware at first of these feelings, but his mind tries to wake him up and to bring him to his senses. It's not personal. It's not the other person that wants to leave him. No. It's he who removes himself because of that kind of negative energy within.

Living with a promiscuous partner

Say you are in a relationship where your partner has been breaking the vows and being unfaithful. How do you respond to that? Unfaithful action is not a problem, but this action is going to become a habit, something that is done again and again. I think to forgive someone is easy, but this person will be tempted into more trouble, until nobody can forgive them. So it's not up to the wife or husband to decide whether to forgive or not. This unfaithful partner will be haunted by his or her unfaithful action and it will make them ugly, and separate them from their partner. We easily become attached to certain actions or habits, if we do them continuously and repeatedly. So actually there's nothing we can do about it. It remains for the person who did wrong to face himself, refresh himself, to be born again, to be in a different environment, the kind of environment that he is comfortable with. He is clearly not on the same track as his life partner.

Should you split up? It's not easy for the other person to change his or her habits. So even though you try very hard to forgive them, it's not you, it's them, and they will do it again. So we see destiny unfolding. Sooner or later, such couples are going to go in different directions. The unfaithful action is only a result, you don't yet see the reason for it.

Unless you remove the reason, it will happen again and again. Until one day you say, "Oh, five years of this. I've had it! Enough". And you move on with your life. You could spend years agonising about why the other person is doing this, but in the end it's their action, and their choice, and their life. Each of us must find our own way, and learn from our own mistakes. We can't reform or change others, no matter how much effort or energy we use to do so.

What about HIV/AIDS and sex?

Of course if you are involved with promiscuous people, or are promiscuous yourself, you are exposed to the risk of HIV/AIDS. HIV is a contagious disease, but we have to know how to remove the cause of that contagious disease. The body is malnourished. We eat the wrong foods - junk food, fried food, frozen, whatever. So that's why our immune system is weak. Our mental strength is also lacking the nourishment of love. So we have the false thought that more sex is needed. Some people in turn, craving comfort, approach anyone sexually, and have this HIV problem and this disease as a result. So people are dying because they are physically not healthy, and mentally they are not complete.

As we mentioned earlier, our first family relationship plays a big role in our happiness for the rest of our life. When people are not ready to marry, but still have children, they land up being parents when they themselves are still children. They don't know how to become loving parents. They divorce, or leave one partner to carry the burden alone. Children are often neglected and ignored in a single parent family, and may be spiritually and emotionally deprived. As a result, some grow up pursuing unwanted and illegitimate sex, catch this disease and are dying, feeling depressed or violent. And this is a vicious circle. So I think we should be educating people well. Just because you are a certain age doesn't mean that you are grown up. It doesn't mean that you have what it takes to be committed to a marriage and to raising children. We need to be wise to be in this 'raising children' business. We shouldn't bring innocent lives into this world from our immature sexual relationships, because we are destroying the world, and people are hurting and people are dying.

Do I need a life partner?

What then is marriage for? A marriage or any loving relationship is to teach us more about love, to help us make loving connections, to help us understand and care for others. We do this first with our loved one, then with our children, and eventually with the world that we live in. Nothing is more important than the selfless compassion that comes from genuine love from our deep inner self.

Do we have a choice whether or not to have a sexual relationship? It's easy to be single and happy, but life will lack that completeness. That means if we have many opportunities to escape and to find excuses not to be involved, not to be committed to a life partner, or some other serious involvement, we can waste our whole life in a selfish search for personal pleasure.

If you emphasise only what interests you as an individual, thinking, 'I want to stay home, I don't want to go out. I want to be with my family. I don't want to mingle,' or 'I want to party. I want to have fun. I don't want responsibilities,' you could still cheat yourself into thinking you have a wonderful life. Actually, good relationships and bad relationships are not the issue. The issue is your personal growth within a committed relationship. There is no reason to avoid a relationship merely to avoid pain. When you have a relationship, you're going to free yourself from that broken mind, so that finally, when you take your last breath and die, you won't say, "I had a lousy marriage because I was separated from my husband." No, you'll be able to say, "That relationship, however it progressed, gave me an opportunity to learn more about love." You have gained some wisdom, some freedom, because you had that relationship with someone, even though you consider it unsuccessful. It's the same at the end of life when you consider your material possessions. Maybe you didn't have lots of money, lots of power, lots of skill, it doesn't matter. Those experiences of living, working and being with others, and dealing with possessions all helped you to develop a pure mind, a clear mind.

Don't avoid relationships

People are lazy. They are also shy, scared, and unwilling to make mistakes. They try to escape. They say, "No, I'm fine. I'm doing fine on my own." But they are cheating themselves thinking they are fine. They need something in life that will force them to go beyond, to transcend. So we *encourage* people to have relationships, no matter what kind of relationship, a job relationship, a life partner relationship, whatever. If you are single you could still fill the role of mother to some child, you could still be a teacher, caring for students. Whatever the relationship, do not avoid it, because relationships are the key to wisdom. But remember, relationships where people are *under the same roof* are the best learning environments. When you live together with other people, you are forced to commit yourself. A life under the same roof with others forces you to see how much you can tolerate. You are forced to stretch, to accept as much as you can accept, to contribute as much as you can contribute. If you only go to an orphanage to visit, oh, you can choose to visit once in a year. If you have some extra money you can give the orphans some money and not even miss it. You have so much choice, and not much commitment. But if you have a daughter who needs to go to school, you have to save money for her. You have to save money for your grandmother, because you love her very much. So you need to have that kind of love relationship to motivate you to contribute more, to commit more, and to tolerate and accept more.

Is it impossible to be single and whole? We are here, on earth, living in suffering. We shouldn't be single. If you consider you are single, you are in trouble. That means there are many things that are not yet done because you are single. Because you can easily walk away from challenges that will grow and develop your compassion. You easily find excuses not to be sincere and concerned and committed. So we are raised to have relationships. We all have to go through that kind of 'relationship-learning'. Even as monastics, monks and nuns, we have relationships. We don't have one-to-one relationships, sexual relationships, but we have relationships in the Order. We live under the same roof, and that trains you to become more committed. We have to learn to tolerate, compromise, and support each other. Even as a monastic you can develop more courage to do good.

I don't think we should encourage people to be isolated, to be confined, and to choose to leave people alone. You should not be separate from people *unless* you are purified already, unless you are *qualified* for life alone. If you are not enlightened, not complete, you do not deserve and will not benefit from this kind of life - alone, single, and away from people.

Second and further marriages, and step-children

These days, many relationships involve children from a previous marriage. There are new people that come with our loved one - step children, ex-wives, and ex-husbands. It's a minefield. So many people suffer so much. What advice is there for second or third or fourth marriages?

First, who is best able to care for the children with love? We should be humane enough to let the decision be made for the benefit of the children. If the mom can take care of the child better, let mom take the child. Don't say, "I'm the father, I have to have custody". If the aunt has a better environment to take care of the children, and she longs to have them, let the aunt, let the uncle. There may even be a stranger who can take care of the children and love them. If you have been in a broken marriage, you must have some sense of brokenness. You have problems in relationships that have not been healed. Then you enter into another marriage, but your character is not yet purified. So you may very well land up in an even more complicated situation with too many step-children all together. With so many egos fighting against each other, it can be a big, big, big problem. Enormous. So we need to have a broader view about love. We need to allow human beings to love each other. Don't ever think, 'I'm the mom. I should just take my child and control him'. Realise you love him, but sometimes a stranger could love and take care of the children better than you could. The courts may say, "You have money. Then you should take care of the children." There should not be a situation where you don't have the right to take care of the children because you're the one with no money, or less money. The children's interests and happiness should be the most important thing. Should the child be going to the mother or going to the father? How do we decide? The mom is in a very difficult situation. The dad is in a very tough relationship. The scariest thing is that the children suffer. *The children suffer*. So we need to see people in a different way. Don't think, 'These are my children. These are other people's children.' And then think, "I could only love children if they were mine. This one is not mine'. Everybody needs to be given the opportunity to love, even though they may not have the right to be with this child, this person.

If you don't know how to live comfortably with your ex-husband, you probably don't know how to be with your children either. It will be a problem. So there is an important role for many people to play in divorced and remarried families, and any families that are short of loving adults. We also need to have more flexible laws to allow loving people to help care for children. Otherwise the house of the remarried couple is just like a burning house, where everybody is scorched by the flames, specially the children.

Other ways to break the cycle

Some people do not find peace and happiness in their marriage or sexual relationship. So they need to find another way to learn unselfishness, maybe turn to the love they have for their children. But in every relationship we need to watch ourselves and our desire to control, manipulate, make demands and destroy happiness instead of creating it. A mother or father who says to their child,

"Because I love you, I have to give you education, so you have to get a degree for me, and you need to do a PhD and you need to become an engineer or a doctor." Is this the way to break the circle of pain and suffering? No. This attachment, these demands, this control instead of open-hearted love makes suffering continue. Same circle, same loop, same rebirth. Again, again and again. So that's why we are never free. Because we are not aware of the behaviour and actions that can help support us to be free.

Chapter 5

Strangers

Living with strangers

When we extend our connections with others, we find ourselves in touch with people who are neither friends, family, nor work colleagues. These are the strangers we meet in other groups or as individuals - people with whom we have not built a relationship. In the moments we interact, we create relationships. How do we deal with these sudden new relationships with strangers? How important are they? How can we understand and relate to strangers? Through our observation of our own behaviour with strangers, we can learn a lot about ourselves. So strangers are helpful in our path to wisdom.

Let's examine our responses. How do we react to strangers in need? When someone's car breaks down on the highway, or we pass a hitchhiker, or we see someone being ill in a shopping mall, how do we respond? Say there is someone needing one or two Rands or dollars at the checkout till, or who doesn't have enough change to pay for a parking ticket, or someone just asking the time or direction. How do we behave towards these strangers? How do we behave to other road users? Are we courteous or rude and impatient?

So many questions asked. When we are involved in such situations we would probably notice that our interests and our needs come first, before we think, "Can we help them?" If we attach great importance to our own needs, other people's needs will take second place. We can see by our response how emotionally strong or weak we are, how clear our minds are. People who are strong and happy in themselves can more easily ignore their own interests, needs or benefits. They have more energy to help other people with *their* needs. This is something we can look at in a detached way. It's not that we *should or should not* help. It's more a question of whether we have the strength to offer support to others. So we therefore examine ourselves, and begin to see who we are, and what we aren't. Are you in need or are other people in need? If you are in need you are in trouble, and are the one who requires help. If you are not in need, other people's trouble will disappear when they are with you, because you are there for them.

Strangers who serve us

How do you interact with other people? How do you interact with those who have a lower status than you, who are working to deliver services to you? Do you find it easy to make friends with the people who serve you? The grocery shop clerk, the bank clerk and the restaurant waiter serve you as a customer. Do you notice them? If you can appreciate their service and value them, and treat them kindly, that means you are very balanced.

Strangers who have power over us

Just because we are polite and friendly and obliging to strangers who have power over us does not mean we are very balanced. We may show respect and have good manners when we are with them but it could be that we are scared of their power, and are not being honest in our manner. Many people are nice to the police. They are friendly to traffic cops. It could be because they are scared of getting a ticket or being arrested. If we are humble with these people, it doesn't mean we are balanced. It could be that we want a favour from them. If we are anxious, or feel pressure, it means we are not sincere. If we are nervous we are hiding some insecurity within ourselves. You can examine yourself and see who you are by the way you respond to strangers. If you can relax and not worry whether you are accepted or not, you are very balanced.

Stranger-watching

The behaviour of people in restaurants is very interesting. Have you ever noticed how people look up when a new person enters a restaurant? When people are more ignorant, they tend to focus more on other people, and the way they look and behave. They see other people as interesting. They talk about people more, analyse them and discuss them. This curiosity comes from the fact that they don't know themselves. As their minds clear they will notice more about themselves - what and who they are. In time, they will include others as part of themselves. So therefore when you see those people talking about others more or using their eyes and ears more to listen to other's conversations, and watch and judge others, that is because they have confused minds. They separate other people from themselves. So they emphasise the feeling that others are not themselves, they are strangers. If we notice we have this problem of needing to look outside, searching outside and watching and commenting on others constantly, it means we are congested inside, we are in trouble. We are not clear. We judge and we discriminate and we are arrogant, and we look down upon others and that is our loss, because they are not others. These others that we look down on are created by the defiled mind, and their oneness with us is ignored by the ignorant mind. But if we are clear and we accept others as part of us, as part of the greater self, then we are richer than those people who, in their ignorance, exclude part of reality – the part that tells us we are all one.

Communicating by phone

Our relationships with strangers present some interesting challenges. Sometimes we need to talk to strangers on the telephone, where we only have our voice to get our message across. It's quite difficult, when we have to use our phone and we don't know the other party. Maybe they are not ready to talk? Maybe they are too tired to talk? Maybe they are too irritated to talk? So we must be very careful when we can't talk face-to-face with someone. We can easily have problems getting our messages across. So we must pay close attention in telephone conversations. We must be ready and prepared for surprises from the other party who may not be ready to talk at all. It is a good idea to cut down telephone talk to the minimum, because there is a great risk of misunderstanding. Nowadays we seldom write. We always try to pick up the phone and call. Maybe the other party is in the car, or not available to talk at all. We need to be understanding, be patient, when we are talking to others on the telephone.

Electronic communication

There are other ways of being in touch with strangers without seeing them face-to-face. There is the world wide web of electronic strangers and potential relationships through e-mail and web sites. How do we respond to the strangers we connect with on this electronic energy network?

We need to remember that we create the world. We create the people. We visualise what they are, who they are, and what the world is – that is all created in our imagination. Remember that what we imagine on the other side of the modem connection is not reality, because we are not real. *We are not clear.* Only a clear mind will realize the reality. The ignorant mind will ignore the reality. Therefore we have illusions. But it doesn't help if we cannot see things without discrimination. Unless we are so enlightened that we can see through the appearances to the truth, we will be putting notions in place when we relate to strangers on the other side of the world, rather than understanding their reality. So don't be curious. Don't be nosy about who or what these strangers are or aren't. Don't imagine what is not there, and then later become disappointed. That disappointment is the price we have to pay for imagining the way things are and getting it wrong. We pretend we know, we guess, and we are misled by our ignorant minds. But one day we have to wake up from the dream. We wake up, and we realize that we want to be in the dream rather than wake up from the dream.

Back to our neighbourhood community

When we leave our computers, we are back to the everyday world of our own community. And there are more strangers we will connect with. Almost the minute we leave our homes, we are in contact with people in the street. A group of strangers that have the power to affect us are beggars. How do you deal with the beggars at street corners? We have been conditioned by society and religion to give to beggars. We give, saying to ourselves, "You should buy food. You should study and get a proper job." Giving this way is very conditional. We do it to satisfy our own needs, when we say, "This money should be used for this or for that." The beggar has a reason to be a beggar. They beg for other reasons as well as because they think they need our money. Some beggars may be very rich, and still beg. Or they may be poor, but spend their money badly. Some people can manage on a small amount of money. But beggars may not be able to manage on their money. There's a reason for the beggar's poverty. We are deluded if we think our 50c or R3 or R30 or R300 is going to be beneficial for the beggar. No amount of money will save the beggar. It's arrogant to think that our one donation will change his or her life. It won't.

The joy of giving

Everyone loves to share and to give. Giving is good for the heart. If you feel you want to give, please give. Don't think that you are giving those cents or dollars to that beggar. You are giving yourself peace of mind, and that's a great comfort for you. Don't think, 'He should get it' or 'He shouldn't get it'. Give to him for your own state of mind, that's all.

It's important to realise that you can choose how to respond. If you feel like giving, why not? But you don't have to give. You are always free to make your choice, in the moment. If you're stopped at a red light, and you have time to give, then do so. If you have already given and don't want to give now, that's OK. There's no right or wrong. Listen to your gut feel. If you feel you want to give, you give. If you don't, you don't. The beggar doesn't expect you to give. Even though you gave, there is the possibility that he will take the money, put it in his pocket, forget about you and your generosity and his hand will go out again at once to the next person. It could be like filling a broken vase with water. So that is why it's important to respond in the moment, and act in whatever way feels right to you then. Relax and listen to your heart.

Strangers in our home

Many of us have a fear of strangers. How do we react to strangers knocking on our door? How do we feel about inviting a repairman whom we don't really know into our home? Today, people are scared to invite strangers into their own homes because they've been frightened by what has happened on the streets to others. They have that shadow of fear in them. They have the reincarnation of people's suffering in them. So therefore it is our common karma that makes us so afraid to offer support to strangers. That is human suffering. That is human disadvantage. People are not able to follow their hearts in wanting to help any more, because they are so frightened of getting hurt as other people have been. That is the tragedy of this world. People have been doomed to suffer continuously through the recollection of past suffering, and past harmful acts. Do whatever you are able to do, whatever you feel comfortable with. It's not your fault if you are afraid to invite a stranger into your home.

Violence

In the cities, violence is a constant fear for many people. If people have suffered violence it doesn't mean that they triggered the action themselves through their actions or appearance. The violent person has been possessed by anger for a long time. An innocent person can bring out that unmanageable emotion enough for the violent person to harm, kill or hurt. Sometimes we think that the innocent person is the victim. In fact the violent person is even more of a victim. He has been loaded with this anger and emotion. We have to realise that before violent people hurt others, they have to hurt themselves. They don't know how to express honestly what they feel inside. Society has educated people to be obedient to seniority without reason or argument. That prepares people to build up violent anger with no outlet. Violent people hurt innocent people at that unmanageable moment. If you have been treated violently, don't blame yourself. There are many causes and conditions to consider, and it is hard for us, with our limited vision, to see the full picture.

Dealing with fear

We may be afraid of strangers. Fear is caused by us not letting go of the imprints of our past experiences. Often our fear is managed in a violent way. Because of our fear we carry guns and hide behind high walls. If you're not letting go, fear will rise up in you. Fear is the same thing as not letting go. You are not wholeheartedly present, so you don't have enough energy to be in tune with the person. You are lacking power. You are not strong enough. That is what we call fear. Lots of energy is diverted to that past experience. Whether you call it attachment, fear, hate, love or jealousy, it is all based on past imprints that affect the present mind. So to deal with fear, we need to examine those past experiences that we have not let go of, and release them. This will help us live more fully in the present, with more energy and compassion to handle experiences that might otherwise cause fear. Letting go of our past and living in the present can make us brave.

Travel and strangers

Business people spend a great deal of time with strangers. They meet their electronic companions from the other side of the world. And they meet others, who may or may not become part of their lives.

What do we do about the lonely married man in the seat next to us on the airplane who thinks his wife doesn't understand him and asks for our e-mail address? It's easy to think that people need something from us. We tend to think like that, because we tend to be the same. Is there something *we* want from the stranger on the plane? Lots of people want to meet again, in order to get something from the other person. Men and women often relate to each other in a sexual or financial way. It seems that the only thing that interests them is sex or money, and that's what they need from each other. But that is not necessarily so. It could arise from the way we are brought up to understand gender issues. We have different genders but have been brought up to see only the difference in gender. We are not encouraged to remember that we are humans as well as being men and women.

We have different body forms as men and women. But our different genders shouldn't separate us from reaching out with our hearts to the other person. Our socialisation and education has sadly not really taught us that. We are often separated into different genders from the time we are little, and as a result we become so curious about the other gender. We don't know them. We are afraid of them and we try to control them. Therefore marriage relationships become more difficult, because the two genders don't work together, they only try to control each other, forgetting they are both human.

Let us get back to the man on the plane. Put aside the fact that you are female and he is male. If you choose to give him your e-mail address, it's not he who is going to harm you; it's you inviting him to take advantage of you. It's not a matter of giving the e-mail to strangers or not, it's what you need or want from them in exchange. If you have a clear mind, you have nothing to be afraid of. If you are in control, nobody can take advantage of you, even though they may want to do so.

Strangers as smoke screens

When we are with strangers, we can pretend. We find it easy to lie about who we are and what we do. We may even think that we can have a better relationship with a new, strange and different person than with the people we know well. We have the feeling that we are escaping the problems in our existing relationships by forging new ones with strangers. We think we can please strangers better than people who know us well. Sometimes we are humiliated by close friends and family. We feel we have been classified as a certain kind of person who always behaves in a certain way. How many people feel they have been classified as a 'bad sister' or a 'mean husband' or a 'selfish mother' or a 'lazy worker'? We have probably all been labelled in negative ways by the people who know us best.

People sometimes want to get away from the people who know and judge them. So they look for comfort and renewed confidence from strangers. You talk to a pretty woman in a nightclub. You chat with a nice friendly man on a park bench. You smile and make conversation with someone in a queue or waiting for a bus. It's good to have a break from suffering by being with a stranger. However, if you keep meeting this person and keep communicating, eventually you will build up a relationship. Sadly, there is a chance that history will repeat itself. You will again be labelled. You will label them. This is the game we play in this world. Strangers are human beings and as soon as we get into a relationship with them, we get into our usual patterns of behaviour - the same patterns we have in our other relationships. As time elapses, the new relationship changes and gets more complicated, because of our egos.

It's easy to think you love someone in the beginning. Your conclusion after a few meetings is, "This is a good friend. A wonderful person! Someone to love!" Because you don't yet have a long-term relationship with them, you are full of hope. However, there is the problem of human impurity. Neither of you is perfect. The past behaviour of both of you will reveal itself again.

Over the years, we change our friends, we change our life-partners, we change our homes, we move into new families, we change the towns or countries in which we live, we change our jobs and our employers. All the time we are searching outside of ourselves for something that we will only find inside. Our egos are giving us problems. The good news is that one day when you are purified you will find there are no enemies and there is no hate or blaming or judging, and you will see that it's not the other person that makes you want to escape, it's your ego.

The first family helps us learn to love others. This helps us break out of this loop of love that turns to dissatisfaction and hate. *When we truly love others, we don't need to escape from them.* A new friend or partner is a short break from the real problem which is the ego, the self that is unable to let go of upsets and misconceptions and past mistakes. Sometimes when you reach an unmanageable state of mind, then travel or a job change or making new friends is very important. Life is like a pond. In a muddy pond, if you stand still and become calm, the mud sinks to the bottom, and the water becomes clear. But if you all keep leaping around, it just gets more and more muddy. We think that we need to keep finding a new pond where the water is clear. Moving away does not truly solve the problem. We think we've found that clear new pond with a new friend or partner or job, but we stir it around and it muddies up again. Every new environment or person is a brief relief, but our egos pull us into the same old patterns. You need to be aware that you bring yourself with you to the new environment, the new relationship. Standing still and being calm may in the end be the only thing that needs to be done to clear the water of the muddied pond.

Giving up too quickly

Everybody needs new chances. There's nothing wrong with change. We all have the tendency to escape. So moving allows us to detach ourselves and gives us more time to understand ourselves. But we take ourselves with us. We tend to be pretenders - pretending there is nothing wrong with us. When we are attached to our past thinking and behaviour, then nothing is solved. The demons are still within us, if we see the same old patterns emerging, time after time.

When we move into a relationship with a stranger, or a group of strangers, we can use this new experience to discover ourselves. We can realise that these patterns will arise again. The real problem is within ourselves. But we need another harbour to help us face our problems, our ego and our attachments. So the new person or group can help us reach a new awareness, if we use the experience wisely.

In truth, strangers are not strangers. If we feel surrounded by strangers, it means that we have limited energy. We do not yet have the ability and power to be connected with the greater self. If we are not strong enough, we easily shy away from strangers. Otherwise we would include anyone in our circle of friends, and not exclude them. If you are powerful and strong you will support and give to strangers just as you give to your family and friends and loved ones. So examine yourself. If you see everyone not as friends and family but as strangers, it means you need to strengthen yourself. You are short of energy. Following a path of increasing calm and awareness, you will recover your ability to be connected to the universal oneness that joins both you and me and all living beings together in a calm, peaceful whole.

Material things

Material things

There are very few people who own nothing. Part of the measure of one's success is one's collection of possessions. There is great pressure on people to own things. This is fostered by advertising and consumer marketing, as well as by one's family, friends and colleagues. How do we deal with the pressure? How do we decide what we need as opposed to what we want? Where is the perfect balance between having and not having?

Those people who have a strong desire to possess something are crying out loud with an unsatisfied need that is in turn possessing them. This craving is hurting them. They hunger for things to satisfy that need. If a person is very picky about how things should be done and criticises and grumbles, he needs to find another experience to fill that need. No matter how well he performs in the future, that hole is there. No matter what has been possessed or owned, it has not brought him satisfaction. So sometimes the collection of material possessions is to fill a hole in ourselves that these things simply will not fill.

Maybe when this child was craving his mother's attention, she was not there for him. Finally, he buried that need deep inside, hid it, and tried to forget about it. In the future he may choose to love someone just like his mother because his need was not filled. Looking for relationships with older ladies – that symptom tells us what could be wrong in someone's life.

When people crave things from outside rather than within them, the pain of that need is like a bleeding wound – it's always hurting. In order to stop it, the person suffering feels he has to treat himself to things, pretending that is what he wants. He is mistaken in thinking something external is lacking. The pain is within, the suffering is within.

More and more

Some women have a craving for clothing – this person is not confident with her looks. She thinks, 'The new clothing will draw attention to me, and make me look better.' The clothing won't really remove the problem. The lack of confidence is inside. If she could simply know, 'I look nice. I look great' the craving would no longer be there. It's the same when craving a fancy car. Maybe the need to buy the car is a result of being looked down upon, or a lack of satisfaction in the past.

Craving may come from the past

We are not born just to this life. We have been here thousands of times, we have been around many thousands of years. There are many previous hurts and cravings and desires that carry over into this life, so we may not see the cause of our cravings and compulsions this lifetime. You may have a habit of dressing up, and it may continue for a long time. Some insecure state of mind invites the attention that you get when looking well dressed and that makes you feel more confident.

The purpose of external things

Monks and nuns wear very subdued clothing. It's a way of reminding practitioners that clothing is an external thing. We are also reminded that this body is like a house, a hut. Your body and mind are a building. You live there temporarily, and you don't take it with you when you die. So we concentrate on not over-emphasising the body. It can create desire and let you lose your peace of mind. Emphasising the body encourages cravings. So dressing simply is a protection to help you from involvement in unwanted action.

Clothing, food, material possessions, a house, whatever, when these possessions serve the purpose of healing a person's suffering for a short period of time, this can also be considered a useful medicine. It helps to calm down that 'disease'. We want to control any re-incarnation into the craving. Sometimes you need to soothe your mind to relieve pressure and lessen anxiety. That's important. If you try to say you're not allowed to own things, it's not helpful. It may cause more trouble because the craving is there. It doesn't help to suppress it deeply because it becomes harder to heal.

As long as you can afford them, you can enjoy your possessions. But if you have to steal money or rob people to own things, that will do you more harm. Lots of people have money and they use it to help people. After you have been buying things, collecting things, say a fine full wardrobe of clothes, after a certain time you realise, 'I have so many clothes. Why?' You start to question your behaviour. You have doubts about the sense in collecting so many things, and start to wonder if that is really the answer.

Let us go back to the example of the woman who collects clothes. It may not be good to collect things, but for a certain period of time, there may be no better way to tame the craving within her. Gradually she will wake up and understand. Everyone has a different journey. Don't think 'I didn't need that collection of ornaments.' You did need it, before, in the past. But one day you realise you don't need it any more. Then you can let go of the collections of material possessions, and grow.

Creativity

Sometimes external things can help your creativity. It could be designing and making clothing, building a house, writing many stories, making lots of pieces of furniture. These products can help a person to show their talent. Maybe you cannot be an engineer but you're a good painter. Painting is a way to help you recognise yourself, find yourself. You see that you are precious, you are wanted in this world. People have different ways to help themselves enjoy what they have to do. This full concentration of doing what you want to do will bring you joy. You open a coffee shop. The coffee and the muffins you serve bring you a great sense of dignity. You enjoy doing something and you want to share it with people.

Material things are not bad at all unless those things do not bring you a sense of peace and appreciation. If they cause anxiety or other bad emotions like insecurity, then of course that should be examined. Otherwise without that exchange of goods and services, people have no way to reach out, contact and support each other. Everybody has different talents, and can share their skills and exchange their products.

Investments or attachments?

How do we put a value on material possessions? You may have an old car. Actually anything is without a fixed price. It's up to the individual to place his or her own value on it. Cheap or expensive, we can decide for ourselves how valuable this possession is. You only need a few cars in your whole life, because cars can last a long time. People sometimes don't want to save money to buy a car. They prefer to spend money on fancy food instead. If you add up the money you spend on food, for instance buying take-aways or eating at restaurants, you will see that buying fancy food is not cheap at all – you can spend carelessly on food.

Of course cars are expensive. But a valuable, dependable car can save trouble and maintenance costs and if you have to pay heavy maintenance costs you will lose more money. Evaluate the importance of a car in your life, save elsewhere if it is a necessary expense and maintain your car and drive properly, and you'll find it's not expensive at all. Compromise, if you don't have the money for other things.

What is most expensive? Think of a house. You will live there for 30, 40, 50 years. You don't have to move. The house can serve you for a long time. And you can sell it – there's usually a high resale value. It's an investment. It will hold its value. Remember we also spend money carelessly. That can add up to a big lump sum in the future. Is something expensive or not? The value of an asset only becomes apparent when you need or want to sell it.

Expanding your living style

Space is quite important. If your family needs a bigger house it's important to consider changing jobs and getting better pay. We don't want to be burdened with financial liability. We are scared to face that challenge. If you are confident, qualified and capable of getting more pay, you can consider doing so if your family will be happier. There's nothing wrong with new challenges, more responsibility. But if you can't make more money, you don't need to push yourself, you don't have to follow everyone else. The decision is difficult. Any decision is difficult. You're not sure. There are always pros and cons. If there's nothing you can do to afford a bigger house, you have to change your mind and enjoy your smaller house.

Rushing into collecting possessions

There is one problem in this world. We rush everything. Everything hangs on one decision. When we grow older, if we have worked hard and invested wisely, we probably have more security, we have retirement funds. But sometimes we risk all we have for one thing. We need to examine our reasons for buying or spending, and relate the cost to our family's needs and our responsibilities.

Handling money, providing for kids

If you have an income, you need to split it into income for spending and income for investing. You need to set aside some money for security, you have to keep some portion of your income to pay expenses. But people take such risks. They invest all their savings in one place to get unreasonable returns. It's greedy. We all want more possessions. But when we have a child, we can't expect that child to grow up overnight. It takes five to ten years to prepare ourselves for having a child. We need to have a financial plan for our children. We need to plan ahead and save for the purpose. We should be careful of taking risks with that money for a bigger return. We need to have some money set aside for risky investments, other money for security and different money for expenses. Plan how you use your money. Give it some thought, because children don't grow up in a short period of time, and looking after our children and their future is our most important responsibility.

Debt Trap

Some people have already made mistakes in handling their money, and have incurred heavy debts to repay. What happens when I am paying back all my income on debt repayment? How do I cope? Well, just remember that it's not *your* money going away. You have to realise the money you are paying back really belongs to someone else already. Every time you make a payment, see yourself becoming free of debts. You are looking forward to a state when you will be completely debt free. That is a joy and a freedom. You are gradually gaining your freedom. Just don't think this money you are paying back is your money. We should appreciate that the bank or the hire purchase company trusted us enough to lend us money. We are now returning it. We will not have so much debt in future, and that is a joy. We are reducing our debt and gaining independence.

Different cravings, different times

In different stages of our life journey we will crave different things. When we are poor, we think, 'I'll be happy when I'm rich.' Before we are married, we think, 'Marriage will make me happy.' When you find out after you have money that you are still not happy, at least there will be less of a burden on you to find money – at least you have diagnosed that. You don't have to crave money, or die for money any more, because you have found out that's not what you needed to make you happy. If you were unhappy when you were poor, then even though you are no longer poor you have built up that habit of unhappiness. So though conditions have changed, you are still enslaved by that feeling. You have felt it for a long time. You carry it with you even when you change jobs. If you are not letting go of that kind of emotion all the time, it is part of the reason for your unhappiness.

Earning money in a way that causes you unhappiness

If you are earning money in ways that disturb your peace of mind, then you are paying too much for that money. You may have given up too much in exchange for riches. Maybe you have lost your family, nature, even yourself by pretending to be what you're not. You do all that for money and lose peace of mind and harmony.

What is the cure for this? If you are rich enough and can afford it, one of the best ways to use your money is to *give*. Giving will revive the mind. Giving is a way of letting go of the desire. When you give, in that giving moment you are so free. Your deepest self will welcome this action. You mind will become more balanced. If there's something bothering you, you can relieve the pressure by temporarily taking some action. Giving is an action that will relieve the mind, it's one way of doing that.

But I worked so hard for my possessions ...

What if I feel I have to give, but I don't really want to? I have worked so hard for what I own, and I can't bear to let it go. Well, it doesn't help to give with resentment. You have to think the money is not lost – it's your contribution to others. You give money to your child but you're really happy to do so, because you feel it's your responsibility because your child is not *'others'*. Your child is part of you. If you think, 'I'm giving and not receiving because it's for others', that won't help the pain inside. That won't help the resentment. Find a cause that you care deeply about. This will motivate you to give more – to AIDS orphans, your respected teacher, some charity that is close to your heart, your elderly parents, whatever arouses your respect and sincerity. Even if they are loved ones, family, you can give generously to them. That's the way to find joy or happiness. Maybe there are some associations whose mission you respect, and you want to help them. Then do so. Don't give to people you hate when you start the practice of giving. Eventually you will be able to give to anybody, any cause, but not now. You will grow into it some day.

When you try to own something, possess something, don't aim at the thing itself, relate it to people. Say to yourself, "I work hard to boost sales because my company's staff need security and opportunity. The children can benefit from their parents' pay cheques." If you can relate your product to people's health, if you can relate it to people, it's wonderful whether you are earning or giving. Money is owned or earned in order to be spent. Do you ever buy flowers for your wife? You're not really buying flowers, you're bringing happiness for your wife. The merchant can go home early because everything is sold, so you are making more than one person happy!

I make money to buy a car for my wife or an educational fund for my children. I earn R20 000 a month because I allow my employees to take home good pay cheques as well. They earn so I earn. That's the principle. If my products sell and my factory runs efficiently, my customers will get products at reasonable prices. It's a benefit for the supplier if I can pay them earlier. If I earn enough money, I can pay my tax, I can give extra money to the orphanage, I can pay my credit card. Earning and spending, you need to think about people first. That will give you power to spend and power to earn. If you think 'I have R30 less by buying flowers,' that's not good.

Cutting back, living more simply

Say you have lost your job, how will you manage with a smaller pay cheque or no pay cheque? It will be a problem if you don't want to let go of your previous status. But if you're in a crisis, you have to think of survival, not status. Realise if you don't have it, you don't miss it. It's only if you want more status, even better status, that you will have a problem in adjusting your lifestyle.

If everyone were to start over again, and forget about the past, nothing would be difficult at all. Many parents wish their child would do well at school, study further and get a degree. Maybe he can't. Hopefully he can get vocational training. But this disappoints them. What do you really want for your child? If he doesn't gamble, drink and swindle people, isn't that wonderful? Release yourself from the judgement of others if you can. Gradually you can adjust yourself to find that balance. If you had a great past, great! Maybe you had a wonderful time till you were 30 years old. But if you want to have an unchanged status, you will hate yourself for losing that status.

Impermanence

People fear change. If we have to be told *'life is impermanence'* it's to wake us up to see clearly that things in the present are not the same as they were before. Wake up! Remind yourself that it's not what you think *should be*, but what *is*. It's not good or bad, changed or not changed. People find the idea of impermanence depressing. Rather remember that every moment is a new moment. You don't try to make it good or bad. Don't worry about 'changed' or 'unchanged'. Just realise that at this moment, everything is as it is.

When we were twenty-year-olds, we had big appetites. We needed R200 for dinner. But we don't crave so much today, so we eat less. It doesn't mean that we need the same money now that we did in the past. In the past you thought money was everything, now you think, 'I have health, I sleep well, I have friends and hobbies, I have all I need.' Before you were restless. Impermanence means that you are happy with different things at different times.

In every state you need different things. You don't need the same thing over and over again. A future job may give you less money but more space and more dignity, and you may have less far to travel. You shouldn't look for the same thing over again. Impermanence is to tell you there's nothing wrong, nothing you need to do or to change. Your ignorance sees it the wrong way, if you find impermanence a bad thing. Impermanence is not a bad thing. Things change, but nothing is changed really. Today is full moon. You thought it was new moon, but it's not. So, it's changed. See it as it is. If you look and see how everything is the way it is, you can just enjoy the present. Change is neither bad nor good. Awareness of impermanence just brings you to a fuller awareness of reality, the reality of now.

Many ways to handle material things

People may think that material things are bad. But it's attachment to material things that is bad. Without an enlightened state of mind, how do people handle material things? Let us think of ways we can relax about material possessions. I can welcome you in many ways, whether I own material possessions or not. I offer you a flower. You see I am welcoming you with a flower. Or I welcome you with my voice. You can use your body action to communicate with people and bring kindness and compassion to their lives. There are many ways of giving, and many ways of dealing with possessions.

Wealth allows us to show we care

If we have an excess of wealth, we can share and give to the poor. How else can we show how much we care? Being rich is not wrong! You can say what you want, but it's actions that count. Someone may say, "If I were rich I could donate more." The test is what you actually do with your possessions when you are rich. It's the greed that shows when you already have a great deal, but still want more and more. Only when you have your necessities satisfied will you know if you are greedy. That's useful information. If you have a family, you want to welcome them, and show that you love them and care about their welfare. So if you have your family or friends visiting, and you don't welcome them by buying fresh milk and fruit, good things to eat, yet you have enough money to do so, it's clear you are stingy, and don't want to share. Your greed is showing.

Wealth can support creativity

In what other way can material possessions be valuable? We can use our wealth to employ different types of creative people. There are lots of architects. They can build beautiful buildings. If a wealthy person hires an architect to build something for him, the architect can create a magnificent building. These talented, gifted people become fulfilled, and have a chance to share their talents for the benefit of others. We need people to buy beautiful houses, to bring the beauty out of the architects. We need people to buy beautiful artwork to bring the creativity out of the artists. This beauty can be preserved for the next generation. You can preserve nature and build art. If we don't see the positive side of materialism there will be lots of lazy people. People could think, 'I don't have to reach out because I don't need it.' We have a responsibility in this world. We have been given so much. We need to exchange what we have with others.

Exchanging skills, services and products

Material possessions and skills and services need to be exchanged. Maybe I make furniture and he grows food. We exchange and we all contribute. As long as you don't cheat people, and don't over-charge, earning a good income is fine. But don't lie. If it's cabbage in the box you're selling, don't tell your customers it's carrots. By exchanging material possessions, by buying and selling them, or commissioning them, the community grows stronger.

If you make a good computer, let the users pay for it. They will appreciate it. Sometimes the price of something tells people, "This is rare. Appreciate it." If cars were cheap, people would just buy them at this or that corner. If cell phones were as cheap as vegetables, people would just throw them away. Material things are part of your mind. Don't think, 'I should do without it'. As long as it's not forced and you have no attachment to it, there's nothing wrong with owning things.

Let talented people show the world who they are. How will people know who this craftsman is, even though he makes some creative craft, if we don't support his work? Artists, farmers, we must appreciate the nature within us and others. We have to live in the village of the earth, and work together to communicate. We have to broaden our minds. Material possessions allow us to meet with people. Sin is not from owning things. Sin is *not letting go*. If you're not letting go, you will have one desire after another. One item of clothing, one hundred items of clothing, till you have to rob to fill your craving for clothing. That is not letting go, where material things are controlling you.

Jealousy of material possessions

What if other people are jealous of my material possessions? When you are jealous of others it's because you are lacking something that those people have. How can you free yourself from the ache of desire? It's only by giving that you can find joy and bliss. That will heal your broken mind. So instead of being jealous, you need to practice giving. You don't have to give everything. It's not giving money away, it's paying your bills in time, being willing to share whatever you have, like your knowledge. Share what you have. Giving is acceptance. You want to give money to the poor beggar. You accept him as you. He needs to eat, you need to give. So you are both satisfied. Giving is acceptance. 'He is rich. I am not.' If you accept the idea of others possessing wealth, and it doesn't distress you, that's also giving. That will make him happy and you as well. It's difficult to lose the jealousy, but you will never be free from it unless you diagnose it and work on healing yourself.

How do we diagnose and heal ourselves?

Often, we don't know about our jealousy. We don't have respect for those people we are jealous of. We hate them for what they have, and want to take it away. So we need to think, 'Why?' The truth is, it's because *we lack the practice of giving love*. If we start to accept them, we will find it easier to release our jealousy.

It's the same in a relationship. A wife thinks, 'I have to be loved'. But she needs to *give* love to counteract that jealousy. Whenever you feel you need to be loved, you need to *start loving*. If you crave money, you must give money. Once you start to care and be concerned about others, you will feel more loved. How do you realise love? If you wish to be loved, *give* love. If you don't practice giving, you will not have material possessions. If you're giving, you are rich. You must have something to give. So as you give, you are gaining. If you don't give you will never appreciate how wonderful it feels. Children need a chance to practice giving. This is very important to their development.

Respect for other people's property

One of the precepts covers respect for other people's property[1]. The precept is to not take that which is not freely given. Practising honesty gives us a feeling of wholeness and decency that helps us become enlightened. It prevents us from doing harm to others. However, in modern society, more and more people disregard this. Theft and stealing are on the increase everywhere. Why?

The pain of stealing

Stealing is the way people tell others there something missing inside of them. People in the old days were hardworking – not rich but very secure. There was lots of love, and people had great confidence that they were loved. Though poor, they shared what they had and gave to others. Today even rich kids want even more than they have. They are greedy, and they steal. They were brought up in such a rich society, but inside they are so scared. They feel unwanted, judged and rejected. They are insecure. Stealing shows there's a big hole in them that they are trying to fill by taking what is not theirs.

After the doors opened to the West in Africa, the African lifestyle changed. When Africans came into contact with the western way of life, they felt lost, empty, useless. Nowadays, they look up to the West and think, 'If I have a house, money, this or that possession, that will be the answer to all my problems.' But it's not. We don't let local people decide what they want for themselves. We see them as 'poor' or 'under-developed' thanks to our intervention. Indigenous people make the mistake of assuming that westerners are better because they have so many material possessions. They think, 'We are so poor. We don't have this, we don't have that.' For thousands of years they were content with what they had and what they were. They had strong societies, with fine values, like u'Buntu[2], the African tradition of caring for others. Today they have lost the belief in themselves they had in the past. They have given up African wisdom and tried to replace it with possessions. In the past, they could enjoy the sun, the animals, the trees and the land. They were rich and wise. Now they are handicapped because they've lost those instincts and their ancestral knowledge. The indigenous wisdom is gone, and they have not been educated to catch up with the developed world.

---

[1] See Chapter 10 – The Five Precepts or Mindfulness Trainings

[2] Ubuntu – a Zulu word that means 'people are people through other people' - the individual is part of a community and interacts through that community, not independently of it.

What is the answer? Westerners and wealthy people have to understand and sympathise with people who are stealing, because there is a cause for that behaviour. We have to remove that cause. We have to help them bring back the balance in themselves, and heal the hurt within.

What if those people are not aware of their own reasons for stealing? They are aware, and they are shouting this awareness by the openness of their actions. They show they are not balanced by stealing. They let the world judge them to be thieves. But lots of highly educated, rich people steal. It's just that wealthy people steal in disguise. They cover up their actions. They condemn these less sophisticated people, who are brave enough to tell the world, "There's something wrong with this society." Civilized people steal from the government. They steal from nature. They steal secretly and condemn those who steal openly.

People who steal openly are unable to see why it is wrong to steal. They were not loved. They have been discriminated against, and looked down upon. They are so used to it, they don't even realise their own pain. They show by their actions that they are hurting. It is up to us who are wiser to realise the cause of crime and theft. Punishment is not the answer. The people who are committing crimes need to feel balanced and worthy. They need self-esteem, and to know that they are loved. They need to be validated.

These people who steal openly have nothing to lose. Why protect their reputations? Even when they cross the street, they don't care about being hit by a car. They feel their lives are worthless. If they die, nobody will miss them. They feel so alone, and they believe that nobody cares. "If I go hungry and get sick, nobody will notice." The father never cared about this child. The mother brings bread into the home, but she is probably not loved either and doesn't understand that this need exists in this child.

Punishment, discipline and lecturing are not the answers to crime. We must give love. We have to help people to raise their self-esteem. At that time we will notice that they will not steal again. They will start to give, because they are rich in themselves.

So, by giving, we heal ourselves. By giving love to those who are unloved, we help them recover, and fill that painful hole inside. By using our wealth wisely and generously we build our community. Practise giving. Practise kindness and generosity. Live in the moment.

Chapter 7

Food? Poison?
Relating to our bodies

Food? Poison?
Relating to our bodies

Watching our consumption and avoiding alcohol and intoxicating substances is one of the five Buddhist precepts[1]. Why is this so important? It is because whatever we take into our systems becomes part of us. We can use this knowledge to heal or harm ourselves. You have heard the phrase, 'You are what you eat.' In this chapter we look at our relationship to our bodies and how we treat them, through what we absorb and digest.

Genetic imprints

First, let us think about our bodies and their health. We all have an inheritance – we have inherited our ancestors' weak parts. I have my father's asthma. Perhaps you have your grandmother's weak stomach. Someone else may have his mother's high cholesterol levels. Although we may not be aware of these problems when we're young, we are more likely to experience them as we get older, because we are born with that potential illness in us. Therapies such as Iridology can track these weaknesses quite early. If you look into a baby's eyes, into the iris, you will see the blueprint to that baby's health. This is the tool iridologists use to diagnose illnesses. Our health is not 'fated' – but we have to work closely with our bodies to avoid the accumulation of poison in those weak parts. Sadly, people don't realise this. Even when we don't have the symptoms of illness, it's a mistake to assume that we are healthy. Even though symptoms may not be showing, the daily accumulation of poison is still there. We have to do cleansing regularly.

Learning to live with our bodies

We do not give much attention to our bodies. We expect them to keep operating, no matter how we treat them. Age, sickness and death come to us all, but there are ways to treat our bodies more kindly, so they will support us through our lives, so we can live in the best possible health. Here are some simple points to guide our relationship with our bodies:

---

[1] See Chapter 10 for the full list of precepts, and their purpose.

Six points for health

❑ Be aware of the ways we can improve our physical health
❑ Feeling the symptoms of illness is helpful, not harmful
❑ How, when and what we eat are important to our health
❑ Regular cleansing and fasting will heal our bodies
❑ We can be gentle with ourselves and our bodies
❑ There is a spiritual side to healing our bodies.

Illness tells us something

Illness is a process of cleansing. Illness is not a bad thing, and we will come back to this later. But we need to cleanse the system once a month, or once a year, otherwise there is tremendous pressure on the body. It's just like cleaning house. If we spend a few hours every day cleaning the house, we don't need to spend four days at the end of the month, and then be too tired to carry out the garbage that we've collected from each room. If I cleanse my system every day, then any discomfort in my system will disappear in a few seconds or a few minutes, or at the most a half-an-hour. But if I suppress my symptoms and allow poisons to build up, I will have hours or days of suffering, as the discomfort grows into illness.

Symptoms of illness

Despite what most people think, to feel the symptoms of illness is good for one. It is beneficial. It means the body is healing the system. When we are healing, we need to use energy for this healing, so we will feel tired. Tiredness is not something to fear. It is helping us to cleanse the system and feel newborn again. After a few hours of this work you will feel tired. The body is continuously doing cleansing work, and you have to support it with energy. Your body needs more energy to cleanse the system when it is very poisoned. When it's loaded with lots of work you will feel exhausted and you will blame the cleansing, but it's not that. It's a process of healing that is very important and not to be avoided.

Healing must be done regularly

We need to eat a balanced diet, so that we get all the nutrients to help us heal ourselves. Freshly squeezed juice is easy to digest and gives the body the energy it needs. Fruit or raw salad is also easier to digest and healthier than heavy, cooked food. It takes fewer hours to be absorbed. This already balances our diet. We will be tempted by the nice taste. When you fry your food, you load it with fat.

If you roast or boil it, you can overcook it and its nutritional value is decreased. So after you have taken in those foods that are already processed and cooked, you will need energy from juice, fruit and salad to help you to cleanse out the toxins left by this overcooked, fatty food. You will get more energy from raw foods and juice to cleanse the spicy, salty, greasy, sweet and sour foods out of your system. If we don't have these raw foods we will suffer.

These days, most food is frozen, or processed, then microwaved or fried. If we eat such food we immediately feel symptoms such as sleepiness. Why are you sleepy? Because your body is taking energy from your reserves to help you digest the unhealthy food you have just eaten. Then you don't feel great, maybe you think you're still hungry, so you eat more, and you feel even more discomfort, which many people confuse with hunger.

What food is healthy?

Are other forms of food besides raw foods and juices unhealthy? Cereals are unfortunately second or third class foods. They are carbohydrates, and are already sticking in your system. Rice, noodles, bread, cookies and potatoes will slow down your digestion. You need more energy to get rid of them. So look to your fresh, raw foods for a balanced diet.

What about proteins? Milk is food for calves, not for humans, but soya is a good source of protein. What about nuts? If you eat too much, you'll go nuts! Seriously, nuts take a long time to digest. Nuts and seeds are for birds. We shouldn't take other species' food. Honey is for bees. Milk is for cows. We need natural food produced from the land, such as fruit and vegetables. Raw meat, by the way, is better than cooked meat. Cooked meat produces acid, and that's bad. No cooked food at all is better. Our bowel is designed for such food – it's such a long bowel, eight times longer than our height. It can digest raw food. The problem with cooked, heavy food is that it sits in the bowel for too long, because it does not have enough roughage to move through quickly. If you let your system sit with so much food for so many hours and days, the whole body will have lots of wind, water and grease.

Nowadays there are so many processed foods. Disregard them. Ignore them. Avoid them. In fact we shouldn't even have refrigerators. Refrigerators allow us to take in lots of unseasonal, imported and processed food. We should consume food that is produced locally, which digests easily. We should eat it fresh, without preservatives. Any additives to make it tasty are bad for the system. If you have those additives you will confuse and congest your taste buds. When you have a dim light, your eye learns to adjust and to function efficiently. If you have a food with a low taste level, you are more sensitive. Our taste buds don't need the additives now placed in foods. Over-seasoned food confuses our taste buds and encourages us to eat the wrong things.

Because of world transportation and storage facilities, foods are never fresh these days, never seasonal. We can buy any food at any time. This is not the best thing for our systems. Local foods are meant for local people. Our bodies adapt to the climate. So we should eat the foods that grow in that climate, at that time of the year. Congested bodies lose power, but cleansed bodies adapt very well to eating local seasonal foods, and find them tasty and nourishing.

Absorbing good food

How well is your food absorbed in your system? Think of pouring a class of water on a thick pile carpet. It will be absorbed. But if you pour the same glass of water on a concrete slab, what happens? It is not absorbed. So, we need to check the quality of our digestive systems. How good is your digestive system? Does it absorb the nutrients? Or does it act like concrete, letting all the nutrients pass right through to finally be excreted, with no benefit to your system? If you have nutritional deficiencies, say you need an iron supplement, you are probably having problems absorbing iron from your food. You are lacking iron because your body is congested, so you cannot digest your food to absorb the iron and other elements. An iron supplement could burden your system even more. Rather cleanse your system, so you can absorb the goodness from your food, and not waste it. Is it necessary to take medicines to cleanse the bowel? What can we do if our body is not absorbing food properly? The best remedy for a bowel that does not absorb nutrients is very simple - juice or water fasting. Don't always depend on remedies. We need to remove the causes, which are poor eating habits and negative emotions. Rest, fasting, drinking only water or juice. This is the best medicine.

Choose the right times to eat

We need to know the best time to eat. In the morning, breakfast is the time for our bodies to eliminate waste. So we shouldn't have a heavy breakfast. A heavy breakfast leaves no energy to digest the food, and uses up the energy we should be using for elimination. Breakfast is time for elimination. Don't give your body a harder time. The best thing to eat at breakfast is juice, fruit or salad.

The best time to eat lunch is when the sun is high. The strong energy of the sun helps your digestive system. Most people don't have time for lunch. Some people think it's too hot to eat at lunchtime. But we should use the sun and enjoy the sun responsibly. The sun is so precious, it helps the system to get rid of accumulated poisons. So eating in the middle of the day is good. At that time your body will prevent you from taking in too much food. If you're healthy, you will realise that when the sun is high, you have a good appetite. The sun works differently in different people. If you sun bathe, it could help to clear the spotty pigmentation on your skin. 'Age spots' are really because your body is not cleansed. Those marks are not the same old marks from last year, they are new marks, because you are still not cleansed. Healthy people are not pasty in complexion. If you are too pale, maybe you need to spend more time in the sun, which can nourish you. Pasty skin means your body is congested, that your body is not well, not absorbing the sun, and not benefiting from the sun so much. In the far Northern parts of the world, people stay indoors most of the time through the long winters and they are pale. They have lots of retained water, and the toxins stored in their system are not breaking up. So their bodies are congested. The sun is even better than food. If you have a good decongested system, you can really enjoy the sun. If you are tired, spend some time in the sun, and see how you feel charged up! But to get back to lunchtime – eat whatever you want to eat at lunch, because it's easy to digest.

After the sun goes down, the energy of the sun is also leaving the digestive system, so its power is reduced. If people need dinner, they need an early dinner. Try to eat your last meal before the sun goes down. It is preferable to go to bed on an empty stomach. Going to bed on a full stomach is bad for you. Eating late at night is very bad. If you eat dinner or supper, you will feel hungry in the morning, but it's not hunger, it's discomfort, because your food has been sitting too long in your system. So the cycle of eating the wrong food at the wrong time will bring your system lots of discomfort. You will kill your system by taking in more food. The answer to these symptoms is simply to stop taking in more food. Most people overeat. Dinner is the time for juice, fruit and salad. Buddhist monks and nuns eat only one meal per day, at lunchtime, and they are known for their good health.

Schedule time to be sick

We need to have regular weekly cleansing. For a few hours or for one day a week, we need to allow ourselves to feel whatever minor illness may arise in order to avoid the major illnesses. We have to schedule time for it. For example for half a day a week, let your body take control. Don't tell your body what to do. If your body is tired or sleepy, lie down and rest. Remember, symptoms show that your body is in the process of healing itself. For example, when a woman is pregnant, at the beginning her body tries to cleanse the system. In the first part of pregnancy, women often feel very sick; they vomit, have no appetite, and may even have diarrhoea. It's the body cleansing your system to welcome the new life. Women don't know that and try to stop the cleansing. They take tablets to stop morning sickness. Some women may experience morning sickness for up to three or four months. Sometimes it continues because they didn't allow their bodies to cleanse, because they were eating the wrong kind of food. If you stop eating, you allow the body to cleanse itself. Then the sickness will go away in a few days.

When a young woman stops having periods, and her body is not losing blood every month, it's wrong. The system's at breaking point. So you need to rest, relax, cleanse, because one elimination channel is reduced. If you don't co-operate with your body, you start to die, easily, quickly. People don't realise that. They try to live the same lifestyle, take hormones, wear make-up to hide their bad health, suppress the systems of elimination. What will happen to us when we do this? We'll get sick more often, take more medicines, more clinical poisons. We will feel desperate because our energy is low, yet we can't sleep at night, become irritated easily, or feel depressed, angry or even violent. It's because we have the wrong concept of illness. Have you noticed how often it happens that people take a vacation, and they get sick? Why do people get sick on holiday? It's because there is now more energy for the body to cleanse itself.

Older people also need time for illness

When you retire, for the first few years your body finally finds the time to eliminate the toxins in it. So you will have more illnesses. Don't worry about it. Listen to your body, and don't fight your system. You will age more quickly unless you schedule the time to respond to sick feelings that may arise in the body. Take orders from your body for that half-day or one day a week. Eat lightly. Have no schedule. Let your body lead you to do what it needs. Are you feeling dizzy? Lie down. You may need some sunshine. If you feel that would be nice, lie in the sun. Allow your body to do its cleansing.

Nowadays people have a busy schedule, and don't have the time for elimination and rest. You do not have time to let your body do its work of cleansing. So you will feel headaches and discomforts in your body. Healing never gets to be done because there's not enough time.

Fasting

The best way to cleanse your body is to fast. It's not only that you don't eat on a fast, but also that you allow your mind to relax. It's not just your food that takes away your energy. Thoughts and attachments exhaust you tremendously. Worry, anxiety, suspicion, and greed – these all take lots of energy from your body. So you need to let go of these. Let go easily. Schedule time to watch what illness arises. The time you set aside for this will allow you to rejuvenate! If you hate your feelings, one day you'll explode. It's the same with the body. Don't keep in your emotions. Headaches, fevers, diarrhoea, vomiting, pimples and boils – these are all an accumulation of physical and emotional poison in your body that has accumulated for too long. Let it all come out. If you don't have this accumulation, it's easy to shake off illness. You don't feel pain or problems. You cleanse yourself quickly, or in your sleep.

A tumour is a cleansing process. Cancer is a cleansing process. Your body collects all its poison and loads it in one place and wraps it up. We don't have the time to wait until the tumour is reduced. Cancer is an indication that we have poisoned our system. We have to correct whatever is wrong in our body and our thoughts. It's no use removing the symptoms without removing the cause. If the cause is still there, you'll develop another symptom in another part of the body.

Fasting is good. Stop eating *cooked* things. Relax the mind. Let no schedule disturb you. It's your body that must set the schedule. Do only minor activities. Listen to what your body orders you to do. This is the time to drink water. Just drink water and freshly made juice, or if you have to, eat only fruit and salad. It's better if you just stick to water and fruit juice. Make your own juice, with no fibre in it. It takes less time to digest pure juice, and this juice can be absorbed quickly, which helps the energy become available at once to help the healing.

Every three months do three days of fasting continuously. After six months, do one week of cleansing. Once a year do a ten-day cleansing. That would be two days eating salads and fruits, two days drinking juice, two days drinking water only, two days drinking juice again, two days eating salads and fruits. Set aside ten days every year. Then you will enjoy quality of life – no medicines, no treatments, no operations, and no chronic diseases. You will probably live as long as you want following this process. And in the end you will be able to eat less and less and die with dignity, with no smell in your body, probably dying in your sleep with no pain at all. We don't have to develop diseases of senility. There will be no blockages in the system that will cause you to easily forget or lose your memory. We can then pass on our wisdom to the younger generation. We will be happy, healthy, wise and confident. These days, seniors live in fear, afraid of poverty. They cannot afford treatments, they're lonely because the family is not around, and they are cared for by nurses. Instead, if you are able to follow a healthy lifestyle and go through plenty of cleansing you will be able to care for yourself to the end of your life.

Meditation on fast days?

While it may seem like a perfect opportunity to add meditating to your 'sickness and cleansing day', don't do it if it takes effort. You can make the effort on other days, but not on your fasting days. There must be no pressure on you or your body at all.

We are all human

Remember we are all human. We sometimes lose control. Don't worry about it. Your body will cleanse at its own pace. Do you have a big party tonight? Enjoy it. Then take it easy tomorrow. We need a social life, and warm relationships with family, friends and companions. Sometimes you will be invited to a party or to have a big meal at the wrong time. Enjoy it with a relaxed mind, then rest afterwards. Don't discipline the body. When you need to spoil your taste buds, spoil yourself. Enjoy special functions, but not every day.

Stressful times

When you are very busy, and have a hectic schedule, it's time for you to eat less. You will have no energy to digest your food. We eat food to nourish the body, so it can reserve energy for later use, so whenever you are busy or emotional it's time to eat less, because there's no spare energy to digest your food. Sometimes when people are depressed they eat more. Why is this, when what the body really needs is fasting? It's because if you take in a lot of bad food, it's like drugging your body. At that time you have too much food so there is no energy for your thoughts. You temporarily escape from the problem. After your body starts healing, the same old problems come back. They were not solved, they were just suppressed because you were too exhausted to think about them. So the problems come back and you escape by eating, drinking, smoking and taking drugs. It's an endless loop going nowhere. We need to be strong to access mental energy. If we are really depressed and worried, we need to eat less.

Athletes and high-performance

If you are athletic and about to enter into a competition, this is also the time to eat less. If you eat more you will take away your attention from your sport, and will be distracted by the food in your stomach. So when you have to go through tests, deliver an important presentation, or face a big physical challenge – any day where you need to be very concentrated, very spiritual, you need to eat less.

Holidays

When you have a vacation, go on holiday, you also need to eat less. Use that time to concentrate on healing.

Whenever you can't turn down an invitation to eat less, you don't want to discipline your body. Remember to eat less the next day. Still, some days you can enjoy food. A good time to eat well is when you're happy and relaxed. Have lots of nutrition to support your reserves, building up for future days, future emergencies. So when you are relaxed, happy and liberated, eat well with your companions. Eat slowly, digest what you eat, and build up your reserves.

Immune systems

People think their immune systems prevent them from getting sick. In fact, the body will never stop trying to cleanse itself. This illness is a way of rejuvenating itself. This rejuvenation is never going to be prevented by the immune system. No system will stop you from being healthy again and sickness is a way of eliminating the poisons that harm you. You must get sick before you can get healthy again. In some systems of medicine, this 'illness' response is a sign that the treatment is effective. In Homeopathy, it is treated as a good sign, not a bad one. So realise that getting sick is the first step towards becoming healthier. Children grow faster after an illness. Once the symptoms have gone, kids have more energy to grow and get healthier. Junk food, too much food, vitamins are more of a burden to your system. Refined food is a burden to the system. Medicine is a burden to the system. They can all slow down healing in the true sense.

Enemies outside the body?

What if your immune system is weakened? It's because you stopped the body from healing. Don't be afraid of viruses and bacteria and fungi. There is no enemy outside the body. A congested system is the worst killer. In an unhealthy body environment, viruses and bacteria can live and grow, just like bugs and fungi infest a weak plant, while the healthy plant growing next to it is unharmed. So the body needs to be congested first before the viruses and bacteria can attack. Some medical practitioners and specialists will give you antibiotics. Those drugs kill not only the bugs but also the healing system. If you don't have a runny nose, the germs stay in your system and sicken you further. If you have diarrhoea, or heavy periods, you are eliminating the poisons. So don't try and stop your nose or tummy running, or stop a heavy period. Instead look at these phenomena as symptoms telling you that your body is sick. Because men don't menstruate, they need a different way to get rid of toxins – they need to exercise heavily, and sweat out the toxins. So these methods of eliminating are a way of cleansing the body, as well as our urine and faeces. But you don't want to be eliminating all the time. That tires out your body. That is why fasting is a wonderful healing tool.

Hunger

Some people say, "I feel hungry all the time. How will I manage my hunger cravings if all I eat is raw fruits, vegetables, juices and water?" First, hunger is not from the stomach. If you have feelings in your stomach that you are hungry, it's probably not hunger at all. It's indigestion. You get indigestion and heartburn when you have lots of acid in your system. The food you have eaten has sat too long to be digested. You feel your stomach needs more food. You grab junk food, chocolate, anything and eat till the pain goes away. Actually you will not be feeling satisfaction, you will just have numbed your stomach. You should not be taking in more food. That message from your stomach is saying, 'Stop! Give me a break! I need to work now, digesting what is here already!" So what should you do? You should notice the feeling in your stomach, and wait. If that feeling goes away, it wasn't hunger. That feeling is a warning from your system asking for a rest. By eating more you are stopping the stomach from digesting what is already there.

The problem of constant hunger means that you need to extinguish the fire in your system. This is very important. We have to know that the symptom is a way of healing. Just like swollen tonsils, a blocked food channel means it is time to stop feeding the system for some time.

Real hunger is sensed by your tongue. Your tongue will tell you, if it's very clean, what it hungers for. The tongue can wait. It's selective. The body will tell you through the tongue what it needs. You may start thinking about how nice some spinach would be to eat. Your tongue is telling you your body needs iron from spinach. If hunger is from the tongue it is patient. That means the body is not congested. But when it's congested, you think your stomach is needing junk food, and you have to eat now. No. Wait. It's your body asking for a rest. Try listening to your tongue once you have cleansed your body a little, and stop listening to your stomach.

Impotence

Lots of men become impotent because their bodies cannot afford to lose any energy, and sexual activity takes a lot of body energy. So your body is giving you a warning. Don't over-abuse the body. You will develop a systemic disease (bone, gland or blood disease) rather than an organ disease because your body is so exhausted and congested from many years of abuse. The body has given up. If you are too strong, too rigid, too hard on your physical body, and stubbornly pretend that nothing is wrong, your body will eventually collapse completely. So take impotence as a sign to rest, cleanse and restore your whole body.

Those who never get sick are either extremely healthy, or extremely sick and are suppressing it. Maybe one day they will have a terminal disease because they have not allowed the problems to emerge and be healed.

Alcohol and drugs

We don't only eat food, sometimes we ingest things that we already know are harmful to our bodies. Why do we do it, and how do we stop? The truth is that drugs and alcohol are just a temporary escape from the symptoms and sufferings of life. Those who drink alcohol feel so excited by it, but they are misled, because the body senses that the alcohol is poison, and it draws energy from its reserves to get rid of the alcohol. The drinker thinks that burst of energy comes from the alcohol but it comes from our reserves that are being depleted.

So gradually those people who are addicted to liquor realise that alcohol no longer gives them the same boost. It's because there is not so much energy released from their body's reserves. They are running out of energy, and running out of health. So therefore they will drink and drink and drink and not get drunk.

What does the craving and consumption of alcohol tell us? It's telling us whoever needs to drink alcohol has a congested system. Drugs and cigarettes are the same, the sign of a congested system, and depleted energy. Alcohol, drugs and all addictive substances make us insensitive, they 'dumb us down'. We are not alive at that moment. The person craving such a substance is in physical and emotional pain and congestion, and the drug fools them into thinking they feel much more life. They cheat themselves pretending there's nothing wrong. This craving is actually just a warning to help us, and to tell us that we need to cleanse our systems or we will develop even more cravings and addictions.

Recovering from addiction

If you are using such substances how do you work to get off them? Can you get off them? Yes, there is a process. We need to allow the body to take time to cleanse, so therefore with addiction you still have this habit of taking drugs or alcohol. We need to remove the cause of that craving. The only way to do that is to cleanse our system and have a good diet, get plenty of sunshine, and have a healthy mind. We need to fast on juice or water, or skip meals, as many as possible, or sweat, or take water baths, saunas and sun-baths to sweat out the addiction.

Is one less mindful because of these substances? Yes, of course. A depressed organ brings a depressed mind. If you are addicted to harmful substances, you may be slow, absent-minded, insensitive, inconsiderate, uncaring, unsupportive or selfish. Addicts are not very healthy physically to start with. As you start cleansing the system, you will have more energy for your mind to support others and give care. We need to help the system to cleanse regularly and not burden it too much. When there is less burden on the digestive system, there is more energy for our attention, our tolerance, our caring, our persistence and endurance. And that is something that is quite important.

The educated mind can block recovery

If your body needs a break, let it rest naturally. Try not to overpower it with your educated mind. Learn to work with your body so it can heal naturally. We are too arrogant to think we know everything about how a body works. So we try to stop the elimination process that we see during sickness, and think we can cure the body. The body has its healing wisdom, as long as we support it, and allow it on its own to heal with time. We will need no medication or treatment. We only need fasting and sunshine. You have lost your voice? You have a cold or flu? You have an upset tummy?

If I were you, I would let my health come back naturally. Eat lightly and rest more. If it takes 30 days to heal, let it. Otherwise the medicine will weaken the body. More unnatural ways of treatment only suppress the symptoms, they do not remove the cause. The 'flu or cold' is not harmful to the system. It is our intervention and interruption in the body's healing which delays the purification of the body. Realise it is cause and effect. Symptoms are not the cause, they are the effect. Symptoms are not serious. They will go away as long as we stop the cause rising again and again. Different climates and conditions will bring out the accumulated poisons within us. Let them out with joy and acceptance. Before long, they will disappear without trace. Then you will enjoy your good health.

Absorbing through our eyes and ears

Besides food and drink, we consume other things. We absorb ideas and thoughts from TV, radio, books and movies. We listen to our friends, family and companions. Should we watch our consumption through our eyes and ears as well as our mouth? Yes. The answer is yes, we should.

Our problem in modern society is that we are too easily bored. We don't know how to spend our time usefully. We don't have deep interests that use our full attention and bring us peace and happiness. We follow trends, rather than listening to our own inner creative voice. This makes us very interested in what is happening in the world. We also look for recognition from society, which makes us scared of being laughed at by others. We watch TV, read books, listen to the radio and visit the movies to find out what's going on, and to be guided on what's acceptable to think and do.

It's OK to be exposed to that sort of information, but we need to balance it with time for ourselves to find our own creative way of living. We have to find and strengthen the hidden peace within us, so we won't easily be irritated or upset by the media or the other messages and thoughts we get from outside.

Nowadays, we need to spend less time on listening to those outer messages. We are addicted to lots of things, lots of thoughts, lots of stimulation, lots of excitement. This constant exposure is harmful to our peace of mind. To protect ourselves, because most of the problems we are exposed to are not beneficial to living beings, we need to cut back on mindless listening and watching.

What should we look for, as we cut back from massive media exposure? What do we fill our time with, instead? We need to have some time alone to listen closely and clearly to our inner voices. When we are alone, we need to look into our minds and say, "What is my state?" We need to understand what's wrong with the habit of not being aware of what we are feeling and sensing.

What about negative speech from our companions? Why do our companions have negative speech? It's because they have so much attachment to the past, and to sensations and feelings which irritate them. So they talk to others about their anger and inner pain. They express their anger to release that pressure within them. That negativity fills them up so there is no space for the present. They are taken back to the past and they are continuously torturing themselves. So we need to be without hurts and connections to the past ourselves, to help them let it out. Sometimes we are not that strong. Then we need to tell them they should let that emotion and upset out at a different time, because those expressions can harm others the way they are harming themselves.

In caring for our body, we can treat ourselves with kindness and compassion. We can listen to what our body is saying, and learn to read those messages correctly. We can rest, and eat fresh, healthy food, at the right times, in the right quantities. When we feel sickness coming on, we can listen to our body, and treat it extra-kindly, with rest and fasting. Gradually, we will grow healthier, and more in touch with our physical self. Gradually we will get rid of the toxins that clog us up and make us less aware and less sensitive. We will be more able to choose *not* to absorb those substances and experiences that cause us physical and emotional pain. Slowly we will become stronger, healthier and more aware. And with this increasing awareness, we will become more aware of our spiritual nature.

The living world

The Living World

We are not alone on this planet. Besides the rest of humanity, we are surrounded by living things – animals of all sorts, from insects to elephants; plants of all kinds from huge trees in massive forests to humble single-cell organisms. How do we relate to the living world? How do we treat other living things? How does our relationship with the planet and all its inhabitants affect our own lives, and bring pain or happiness to us?

Independence

We have talked about independence before. Humans have a strong urge to be independent. The truth is that we need to realise our dependence on others in order to reach the independence we so crave. We cannot live an independent life by separating from other living beings. So, the first thing we need to realise is that we are dependent on nature, on the creatures and beings around us, whose living energy helps us survive.

What is nature?

What is nature? We tend to think that nature is everything that man has not created – living things that grow without our involvement, as opposed to the concrete skyscrapers or motor cars that man has built. Let's look at the word 'nature' a little differently. Think of nature not as 'other living things' but as *reality*. Nature is what it is. Think of it in terms of 'the nature of a tree is to grow branches' or 'the innate nature of a dog is to bark'. In other words, nature is the way things are. Our biggest mistake is not to be open minded as we look at nature. We need to observe the nature of things *in the moment*, which is observing without making assumptions, seeing things as they are rather than as we wish they were, or how they used to be, or could be. Because we are not being here, in the moment, we don't really understand the nature of a tree. We need to understand that even beauty is not the same all the time. At any moment we need to be awake, we need to see the changing reality, the way the world is right now. We are in reality, in nature, every moment. Nature is never separate from us. Everything is all connected. You need to be fully conscious to give nature your full attention. You need to be open minded to realise nature, to realise the way things are.

We look at other creatures and don't see their real nature. We don't see a bird or a cat or a tree as what it is, but rather as how it will benefit us or get in our way. We don't see the dog's or vegetable's or flower's true nature, because we see them from a human point of view. We see the 'human' tree rather than the 'tree' tree, the 'human' animal, rather than the 'animal' animal. We have a notion in our heads that animals and plants are inferior to us. We see animals as possible pets, we assign motives and values to them that they may not have. We see them as subordinate, and we see them from our point of view only.

Relationships with other living beings

If we are not careful, we can use our relationship with the living world as a form of abuse. We feed birds with baked bread, feed dogs with dog pellets. Those are not what they eat in their natural state. Wild birds and dogs do not eat man-made food. We make them do this when we keep them in our homes, because we do not appreciate their true nature, and we don't treat them according to what their true nature requires. It's the same with plants. We select the ones we want, plant them in flower beds or vegetable gardens, manipulate them, give them chemical fertilisers and create new kinds of plants. That is not the nature of reality.

Take our relationship with pets. Dogs bark, and we think, 'This dog is not trained'. The dog is obedient so we pat it. Only the behaviour we approve of is valued, even if it's not the animal's true nature. We grow plants that produce bigger vegetables, so we can make more money. We grow flowers that have bigger blossoms. But we don't really examine the results of all our meddling with nature. That's why we suffer from a lot of unexpected results – drought, floods, pollution, and population problems. We treat nature as beneath us, not worth considering, not worth closely observing. We forget that humans don't control the whole planet. All living beings provide balance and work together to keep the planet in balance.

Human excess

We have refrigerators so we can store excess food, we grow too much food in some parts of the world, we emphasise productivity, adding chemical fertilizers to grow more, faster. This is human interference. We are seeing things from our limited human point of view. We don't see the damage to the soil, the nutrients that are missing in the crops through thoughtless human intervention. Our masses of agricultural produce, that we engineer to grow 'bigger' and 'better', have lost their taste and sweetness. These vegetables, grains and fruits have no flavour. Because we can store lots of resources, we waste things. We don't realise that we can't keep up this production and increase it forever. There will be a crisis one day because we have wasted natural resources thoughtlessly by creating produce in an unnatural and greedy way.

What is the answer? First, we need to look at our viewpoint. We cannot view things only from one point of view, from one nationality or sex or economic system. We need to be open-minded to the awareness that there is nature in everything. We need to understand the value of floods and droughts, understand why they occur, and what causes them, and what conditions must be there for them to happen. There is value in everything that exists. We should be wary of saying, "This I need. This I will get rid of." This applies to living beings even of the order of the virus and bacteria. We say, "This is a virus. We must kill the virus. These are bacteria. We must kill bacteria." Rather we should be thinking, 'Why is the virus here? Why are bacteria here? Why is the insect here?', because there's a reason for them to be here. There is value in their existence, even as there is value in the existence of all other animals and plants. Nothing is unwanted. Bacteria and viruses stimulate our immune system to become stronger. There is a place for everything, a role for everything.

Killing

We are in this world because we are like it, impure, imperfect, full of suffering. This means that we have floods, droughts, earthquakes, death, diseases, and disasters. Some sages consider that these things are created by our impure minds. Certainly humans have been responsible for many 'natural' disasters – floods caused by badly constructed dams and hillsides stripped of forests, droughts caused by destroying the natural vegetation, over-population and over-grazing. Some holy books have predicted disasters because of man's inhumanity and savageness. As long as we have impure people we'll never stop the natural and human disasters from occurring. We can only try not to kill, and not to harm human beings and animals. But as long as there is one single individual who is not purified, the harming and killing will always happen.

We kill when we are walking – we tread on ants and insects without realising it. When we drive our car on the freeway, we kill the insects who die on our windscreens. When we suffer flu, our antibodies kill bacteria. Our bodies kill viruses, bacteria and fungi, or we use poisonous medications to do so. We spray insecticides to kill cockroaches, bugs and fleas. We put down rat poison to kill rats and mice.

There are few real animal rights. We kill animals' natural power by keeping them in places that are for people. That's a way of killing too. Animals need to be out in nature.

It's a world of fighting. Everyone fights to get their own space. I want to live and you want to live. I fight for my own space. We do not live in harmony. We are separate from nature, from other beings. So everyone fights for their own space and killing is inevitable. The tiger kills, the snake kills. Humans also kill. Maybe not physically, but we kill people's rights, their confidence. We destroy their space, their chances, and their opportunities. As practitioners[1] we have to accept the fact that this is *samsara*[2] .

What can we do about killing?

We should promote less killing. Expecting 'no killing'? That's impossible. People easily spray and kill ants inside their houses. But then we can suggest that they don't kill the ants in the garden or the park. Beings need space to be free. If we take care of our bodies, we don't have to take medicines to kill viruses, and bacteria. So that is prevention.

If you are healthy you will appreciate a diet of vegetables and fruit. If you're not healthy, you will have a strong need for meat and fish because your system is poisoned. So we eat meat, chicken, fish and seafood and someone has to kill them so we can eat them. If we are healthier, we cause less killing. It's difficult to become a vegetarian if you are not healthy.

Finding our place in nature

In order to be at one with nature, we need to see it as it is now. The wind blows. The sun shines, the rain falls. That is as it is. We always want more sunshine, more rain, more wind. Whatever the weather, it's a bad climate from our point of view! This is where we make a serious mistake. The climate is the way it is. If we can enjoy it the way it is, we will be happier.

---

[1] *Practitioners – those who practice following the Dharma, or Buddhist teachings.*

[2] *Samsara – The cycle of existence. Day to day life in the cycle of ignorance and suffering.*

How should we be treating the earth?

We are creating deserts on this planet. We need to let the land rest for some time, instead of pumping it full of chemicals to cover up the problem. We need to allow insects and other creatures to be there because that is reality. We need not kill insects, because the system will balance itself. When we interfere with nature we do so without realising the full consequences. Every time we interfere with nature we get intended consequences and *unintended consequences*. We put the system out of balance because of our lack of awareness of and lack of care concerning the outcomes of our actions. Our own body systems need to be balanced, and so does the planet.

Understanding the nature of balance, and the balance of nature

We have to accept that whatever is in the system has a right to be there. We shouldn't try to feel superior and think the bacteria are intruding and not wanted. Bacteria will never continuously harm the system. In order to balance life on the planet, don't blame the bacteria, or change the environment. Should we kill insects? Take cockroaches as an example. Why do cockroaches come into a kitchen? It's because there is food lying around, stale food. Cockroaches like kitchens that are not completely clean, because they find plenty to eat. If you keep your kitchen very clean, and pack away food in containers, there is nothing to attract cockroaches, so they go away, because there is no food to help them grow and breed. If you kill bugs with insecticide, the weak ones will die. But the strong ones may not, and they may breed into a more powerful, more destructive insect. This has happened with mosquitoes. Chemicals that used to kill mosquitoes no longer work any more, and malaria treatments have become ineffective. There are bacteria in hospitals that are immune to most known antibiotics. There is a strain of multi-drug resistant TB that is immune to the treatments that used to work in the past. These new creations are as a result of our intervention, without awareness of the unintended consequences of our actions. Termites love rotting wood. There is a reason for termites to be eating that wood – it's because the wood is in that condition. That is nature and that is reality. So, in order to prevent termites eating our wood, we need to keep the wood in a certain condition. Termites will eat decaying wood, just as sure as dogs will bark.

Examine the causes and conditions

Sometimes nature scares us with swarms of locusts, huge flocks of finches, plagues of caterpillars. Instead of reacting without thought to stop theses things from happening, we need to see what is out of balance in nature that has caused this over-growth. We need to look at why it has happened, and be patient to allow the balance of nature to correct itself. As a body may take years to sicken, so it is with the planet. It has taken many years to sicken, and will take many more to recover. There are no quick fixes. If we interfere without thought, the solution can become the new problem.

The planet is not here just for the benefit of humans, or for our commercial interest. We need to see the whole planet as a living being, and treat it with respect. The need to have this factory to produce this product at this price means we ignore the environmental issues. We spend too much time looking at the benefit for humans, and not enough time realising that as human beings we need to consider the benefit for the whole planet, and all the creatures on it.

Nature and living in the city

It's more difficult when we live in the city to understand how we link together with all other forms of existence. For the ordinary person, without realising that nothing is easy without interconnection, he takes it for granted that water comes out of a tap, that toilet paper is there, that air-conditioning keeps the room cool, or heating keeps the room warm. He does not realise that there is so much more to water than turning on a tap, more to garbage disposal than emptying the trashcan. People in the city will never enjoy a really good quality of life if they think money can buy whatever they need. They will never appreciate the importance of fresh air and clean water. They casually pollute the environment, and waste natural resources. If a city is getting help from each individual living in it, it becomes a great city. As ordinary people, we need to realise that any action of ours affects the whole world. Every time we litter, or spit, or burn trash, or leave the tap running, we think that it only matters in our own yard, it only affects us, and it's only our business. No. It affects the whole planet. The individual is the whole world. If you start examining your own actions, you can have an effect on the whole world.

Living beings have needs

We need to be in touch with other livings beings to understand their needs. We need to touch water, and the earth, and animals and plants, but sometimes we touch them without feeling any connection, without bringing our attention to their own reality. We tend to use them mindlessly. Why do you have other living creatures in your life? They are there to help you connect with all life. You have a plant in your house, and you use it just for your own personal pleasure – you enjoy looking at it. How about using that plant to understand the nature of plants better? Notice the plant. Feel its energy. Give it attention in the living moment. Care for it with love and awareness of its needs. It is through learning to care for other living things that we become more alive. We need deep, close contact with people, animals, trees and plants. Those contacts bring us into unity with life itself.

Pot plants

Are pot plants silly? Should one grow plants in one's flat in the city? Pot plants are not silly, as long as you can learn from the plant, and watch it deeply. For instance, you can feel that the plant is dying from the polluted city air. You can see how your love and attention helps the plant grow. You can learn how much sunlight and water your plant needs to stay healthy. It's a lesson to you as you watch the plant changing, growing and dying. Becoming aware of what the plant needs, we learn to be 'no ego' or 'no-self'. We learn to *be* the plant. This applies to all aspects of caring for the environment. You see your swimming pool's water is dirty. You start to take care of the water in that swimming pool, because you see what it needs to be clean and pure. It's not that you are *fixing the problem*, it's that you are *feeling what the water needs*. That is what is important, putting yourself in the place of the water, becoming one with it and understanding its needs.

Pets

Children need to learn how to appreciate other living beings. In the beginning, children can be arrogant, thinking, 'I love my pet and that's enough'. Then one day they will realise that the dog or cat is as important as they are. Having pets is the first step to becoming one with other living beings.

We can become attached to pets and pot plants. If you are attached, you will cry when your pet dies or your plants wither, but to gain wisdom, we need to move away from this needy attachment to feeling compassion and detachment. We need to loosen the cravings that make us want things to be different than they are. You may want plants that will be everlastingly green. That's against nature. Nature is the way things are *now*. In winter, the trees are bare. In spring, they blossom. Now it's dry, now it's cold. Things change. Realising that *change is the nature of reality* is a trigger for your enlightenment, and builds your mindfulness.

Should we have pets?

Not all people have families, and we did talk in earlier chapters about the value of pets in teaching loving kindness. It's important to have someone or something to love and to care for every day. What about people who travel a lot but would like to have a pet to love? Well, everybody is different . Everybody is responsible for their own lifestyle. They decide what they want to do. If you have a pet to enjoy 'when you have time', you will not fully benefit from having a pet. If you have a choice to fully appreciate a pet all the time, why put up with less? Stop your travelling and get a pet. If you can have a healthy mind and wise attitude, you will benefit from being with living beings everywhere. When you travel you can still appreciate how the pets give you joy when you are with them. You will learn to appreciate living beings when you see dogs and cats and birds out there in different places and countries. They will be helping you to be happy with other beings in place of your own pets. They will be there everywhere for you if you see them as living beings.

There are other issues around having pets. If you are interested only in your own dog and no other dogs, having the dog could become a burden. We need to allow this dog to be with other beings as well. The dog also needs to be able to have attention and care from other living beings. We must be careful of this addiction – becoming addicted to a pet can be similar to other addictions.

What about people who treat their pets like children? Well, each of us can have a different view of the same thing. You can call your garden or your computer or your pet project your child. If you don't have children and have lots of time, you may want to devote time to these other things because they take as much time and care as a child would demand from his or her parents. Don't think however that we are treating our pets wisely when we treat them as humans. We may be humble to be with our children, but we can be arrogant with our pets. We give things to our pets for what we think is their benefit, but we are actually abusing and controlling them. The end purpose of bringing up any child is to help him or her to become adult and independent. But do we do that with our pets? It is too easy to make our pets dependent on us. They miss us when we are not around. They are lonely and unhappy. This unhappiness is caused by us. A dog is a dog, and a bird is a bird. In the past they were once wild animals, adapted to their environment. Nowadays they can only survive on pet food, and indoor temperatures. We raise children to be independent, free and strong, not dependent and attached to us. In the same way we should be mindful not to allow our arrogance to let us to spoil our pets to the point where they become little more than "toys" rather than living, free creatures.

Living in the city

From our homes, we reach out to the wider world, our community, our village, town or city. Not all of us can live in the country. Many people these days live in huge cities. Some people hate living in the city. They hate the traffic and the concrete and the pollution. How can we learn to live happily in the city?

If you hate living in the city, first, ask yourself, "Why am I staying here?" Why stay? Go away. Look for another job somewhere else. If you don't let go, and move away, you won't find out what is causing you pain. This doesn't mean that there's a problem with the city. It's a problem in yourself. Get away from the city and find out what's really bothering you. Be honest about the problem.

Whether you live in the city or the country it's the same. You need an open mind. If you see the city and country as different, and discriminate against one or the other, you will be unhappy. The city is not just the city. The country is not just the country. But if you don't see it like that, don't suffer. Go away and you will realise it's not the city's problem. The country environment will bring out what is really bothering you.

Enjoying nature in the city

How do you learn to enjoy nature? If you only have a small yard that means you can learn to enjoy the public park. Your yard can become wherever you are passing by. Appreciate what is available with your heart and eyes. In nature, wherever you are, learn to feel the living beings around you. The flowers are talking to us, complaining to us. Listen. They will help you talk to the big garden of the neighbours. Start with your tiny yard and your tiny plant and your little pet dog, to get you started in communication with plants and animals. Then you will more easily be able to communicate with bigger yards and gardens, and enjoy more and more living beings, till you are in touch with the whole living world.

It's easy to live in the city and enjoy the city. Reality is beauty. We need to see the beauty in the reality. Only with an open mind and a clear heart can reality be observed and realised. Don't see city buildings as 'not nature'. You can feel life in the paint, the concrete and the steel. There is energy in these things as well. The aspects of the city are from the country, just in a different form. The buildings are made from concrete, which is made from gravel, sand, limestone, bauxite and water, which are all part of nature. The steel is made from iron ore and carbon. Iron comes from rocks in the ground, just in a different form. It's part of the earth. You don't have to have a dirt road to feel its nature. You can feel a tarred road instead. You can feel nature in the freeway. It's also rough or smooth, hot or cold. Be neither addicted to the country or the city, because in essence they are the same.

Civilization

What is civilization? *Civilization is a clean environment, wise people and a simple life.* People may say that Africa is not developed, not civilized. But what is development? It's not necessarily high tech, high-rise buildings and materialism. Human civilization exists in the three things listed above. We need to think how we can add these to our lives to bring more civilization to our communities, rather than thinking that because we have wealth and material possessions and power that we are civilized. Let's examine the three elements of civilization …

A clean environment

A clean environment is an important part of our lives. Seventy-five percent of our bodies are water. We have to take in produce from this universe daily to stay alive. We need water and sun and food. The soil is going to grow our produce. We all have to breathe in the air to rejuvenate our bodies. Soil, air, water. Those are essential parts of our precious life, but we easily ignore them. We have to drink bottled water, and have our air conditioning running to remove the toxic fumes in the atmosphere. We try to get away from the city to live in the suburbs where the air is cleaner when we go home. But we can't wait till night time for fresh air. We will be dizzy and sick without clean air. People can eat meat or fish, but without rich, fertile soil to produce food to feed the animals, we will not survive. We eat poison because the animals we eat are being poisoned. Even vegetables and grains are damaged with insecticides and man-made fertilisers. It's a circle, all linked. Food is linked, like we are, to the soil. One day we will become ashes to feed the soil that feeds the plants. We cannot ignore the need for a clean environment. We cannot have imported products in our life and ignore the pollution around us, and still think we are developed and prosperous. We nourish each other. We must nourish the environment as we nourish other human beings.

Wise people

What is wisdom? Wisdom is the realisation of what is happening. Wisdom is not lots of knowledge. What is the point of knowing how to solve problems if you can't figure out what the actual problems are? Wise people answer the calling of circumstance. Wisdom is seeing the reality and then responding. Wise people help make life more pure and more simple, they cut through the complications.

A simple life

What is simple? Don't try to get complicated. Simple is *as it is*. Sometimes we don't see the trash, we don't see the pollution. That is not leading a simple life. Leading a simple life is to encounter reality as it is now. We make life complicated because we are confused, and we refuse to look at things the way they are. If your mind is clear, reality is simple.

We delay handling problems because we don't see them. Take the example of eating poisoned food. Who wants to do that? No-one will. So life becomes complicated if you don't see what you are eating, if you don't realise that this processed or contaminated or poorly grown food is really poisonous to you.

There is much less chance of misguiding our children in our schools if we lead a simple life. Children need wise and simple guidance. But today, children at school are often not raised in wisdom. We are so surprised when we see how our children turn out to be. But we have only ourselves to blame, because we do not teach children the simplicity of life by getting them to observe closely the way things really are. Life is only complicated because we don't see the reality.

Reality is never the same, it changes. The flower blossoms and withers. The sun rises and sets. Reality is continually changing. We let the reality escape from our presence. We don't see things happening and changing, new realities existing all the time. We should not let the moment slip away, but see it as it is. *If you see the world and the situation as it is, you can make changes. You can do something about it.* We need to adjust life to find the middle way, the way of least harm. We can always change things. There is so much we can do. I can, by clever observation, see what I can do to help meet the needs of the planet. Closer to home, I can see the roof is cracking, the building's paint is peeling, and get it fixed. If I listen and watch closely, I can answer the prayer of this or that living being and make things better for it.

A simple life doesn't mean giving up using soap or shampoo or doing without beautiful clothes. That is not a simple life. A simple life is to appreciate what is available now, but not to be owned by it. It is to enjoy and appreciate whatever is available. Before you lose them, you have to appreciate them, but you need to realise that they will be gone one day. When the tea is hot, drink it. When the milk is fresh, drink it. Don't try to always keep the tea hot. That's too complicated. Eat your vegetables when they are fresh. If there's nothing available, you have to accept that's the way things are now, but things will change. Today there's no coffee, but there's juice. Enjoy the juice. Don't miss your friends when you are with your children. Enjoy your children. Enjoy your grey hair when you have a grown son or daughter. Don't try to feel young when you have a fifty-year-old son. That's the simple life. Living in the moment.

Just as you can't use all your possessions at the same time, be ready as things change, as the milk sours, and the money disappears, let them go. Don't cling to the past. The simple life is not getting rid of your money or giving up your big house and car. Enjoy them. Just be aware that conditions will change. Money not spent now may not be there in ten or twenty years' time. You can spend it or keep it. Do whatever you choose to do in the moment. That's the simple life. Clinging to things, being afraid of losing them, not seeing them as they are - that is the complicated life. A wise person can live a simple life, even though she is very rich. You don't have to be poor to lead a simple life.

Equanimity

In being wealthy, there is the danger of arrogance. We should not, being rich, look down on the poor person and feel pity and despise them. When we are rich, we may think that our poor neighbour is suffering. But maybe they don't feel that way. If we have power, we think we can control people. We are proud of ourselves. We look down on others. No, don't do that. We look at a dog and think dogs are sad, they don't have what we have. No, don't think that. The dog may be very happy to be a dog. The poor may have chosen to be poor, and to live that way. Their choice is not our choice. Wealth is not better than poverty, it is just different. We will feel happier in ourselves if we can cultivate equanimity, which is not just being calm and tranquil in the face of all circumstances, but also being able to see everyone as equal, without discriminating between ourselves and others. Equanimity is one of the four immeasurable minds, or divine abodes taught by the Buddha[3].

---

[3] The Four immeasurable minds are: Loving kindness, compassion, joy and equanimity. Meditating on these qualities brings us great calm and peace.

Some Buddhist teachings say that if we behave badly, we may come back as an animal rather than a human being. So many people who believe in reincarnation may be very afraid of being born as a dog and judged by humans. We need to be careful of using that philosophy to consider dogs and other animals as inferior to us. Just because a being is a dog doesn't mean that he is worse than a human. Having been born in the human realm, you may consider being a dog is bad — that's purely your point of view. From the Buddha's teaching, we know that humans have this weakness to want to dominate and control, and they think that to be born as a dog or a bird is to be enslaved by humans. So there is this discrimination in some people's minds. But if everyone could cultivate that oneness within them, they could be one with the tree, one with the dog, one with the water or the air. So a dog is not a dog any more, and a tree is not a tree anymore. In Buddha's mind, there is no dog, no tree, no bad, no good. Our efforts must be to get rid of such discrimination. We all have oneness of mind within us. We all have the Buddha within. Nothing is inferior or superior, weaker or stronger, better or worse. We are all part of each other, in one living universe. When you feel yourself separate, isolated from other beings, you are in the circle of suffering, giving, receiving, and never free of becoming[4]. Our freedom will only be realised when we are no longer separate from all other living beings. Human bodies are really like containers. We have different containers but we are all the same essence. Juice, water, soup. The containers are different. Even the contents seem different. But if we realise the contents are the same, the container doesn't matter any more.

---

[4] The Four Noble Truths explained by Gautama Siddartha show us a way to break free from the cycle of becoming, of births and deaths, through following the eightfold path that leads to enlightenment.

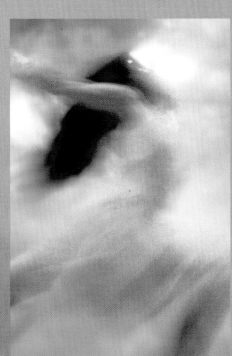

In touch with the spirit

In touch with the spirit

Once we have examined our relationships with others and the world, many of us are still left with questions. We search for answers in religion and philosophy and try to find reassurance that our lives have value and meaning. How do we relate to religion and a belief in God, Allah or a Higher Power? How do we explain the unexplained, the intangible and the un-manifest? How do we deal with our longing to be one with the universe?

Understanding our religions

Sometimes people find it hard to be what is described as a "Good Catholic / Protestant / Jew / Moslem / Hindu". How can they improve their understanding of their religions? The truth is, if we need religion, we are not considered a good Dharma practitioner. Religion is for people who need purification. Don't try to be a good Buddhist when you are still learning from your religion. Accept who you are. Don't try to be good. In order to decide what is good you move into being judgemental. Are you humanly good? Or angelically good? Or animally good? It's just a question of point of view. We need religion to nourish our humility for today's practice, because we only have today, this moment, now. If you let this moment slip away, you don't have life, because life only occurs in this instant. Your religion is for you to live this moment fully, because you are humble. Don't even think about whether you are good or not good. That brings pressure and arrogance.

Do I need a new religion?

We need to have many different religions for different people in different places at different times. Religion is not the truth. But religion helps us open and clear the mind. Truth is in your state of mind. So why bother to find a new religion? Let your current religion help you free yourself of your ego. No matter what religion, there is one truth. You will realise that with an enlightened mind.

Human versions of the truth

Sometimes people are very confused by religion. They may want to change religions. What does it mean to be Christian or Jewish or Moslem or Hindu or Buddhist? We are all from different backgrounds. The reason we have a religion is to liberate and purify the mind, to cultivate this freedom in the mind and to have it under control. The religion of our country or time or culture works to help us do that in a way we may be able to understand.

Lots of people believe in God. What is God? What does God mean? God is beauty. God is compassion. God is wisdom. God is reality. We are Christian or Buddhist or any religion, but no matter what teaching you believe in, there is only one truth. It does not matter that your understanding of the truth is a different version to mine. Both are human versions, ordinary versions of the truth, not the truth itself. That is not the truth that Jesus Christ tried to teach us. That is not the truth that the Buddha tried to teach us. No matter how hard they tried, they could not get the message to us, because we cannot access our Christ mind or our Buddha mind yet. Because we don't get what the truth is, we think religions are different, that some are higher or lower, and we fight against each other. That is wrong. That is because we don't have clear minds.

Because of our defiled minds, everyone has a different version of the truth. So now our point is not to change to a religion of a different name, or adopt a different faith, or to change to a different God. We need to make it all one within us. Everyone has the potential for that oneness, that clearness, that openness of mind. That is the purpose of religions. It is OK to have many names for different religions and different faiths, but we have to realise that religion itself is not the truth. It's OK to have different methods and ways, but don't cling to the methods or cling to the ways. Ways and methods are not the truth, they only help us to realise the truth.

If you are a Christian and you are defiled, you cannot see the Lord. If you are Buddhist and you are not selfless then you cannot see Buddha. With this kind of defiled mind, you try to fight against each other's religions, but in doing so, you move away from God, away from Buddha. You're not going to be close to God or close to Buddha if you are fighting or in conflict. If you are a Christian and you cultivate that great love towards sentient beings, then the Lord is in you. If you are Buddhist and you cultivate that selflessness and egolessness, then Buddha is in you. No matter what religion you have, your obstacles are ignorance and attachment. So don't misunderstand religion. Religion's only purpose is to help you balance your mind, clear your mind and free your mind. If any religion cannot bring you this peace of mind, then you cannot blame the religion. It's not the religion that makes you confused. It's because you don't realise that the problem is within your own mind. You don't have the right attitude, the right view within you. You need to balance your mind and move away from extremes to reach the middle way.

Different Practices

People chant the Buddha's name. What is the Buddha Name practice for? It is to cultivate awareness, cultivate mindfulness, cultivate enlightenment. When Buddhists chant the compassion mantra, it is to cultivate the great compassionate heart. When we prostrate to the Buddha, it's because we want to cultivate that tender heart, that humble mind, that soft heart. There are different practices in different religions. If you don't pray, God will not punish you. If you don't bow, Buddha will not punish you, because the God and the Buddha are selfless, they are kind and fair and gentle and that means the punishment is not from them. Punishment is from our own ignorant minds.

Two religions?

Students ask, "How can I have two religions?" If you think you have two Gods you are not clear and open. What is serving the Lord? Serving the Lord is simply the cultivation of honesty, kindness, fairness and clarity. If you have an open and clear mind, you serve the Lord Jesus or serve the Buddha, by always being just, kind, gentle and compassionate. There is no contradiction at all. If you go to church or to the temple, it is in order to cultivate that selfless devotion. Afterwards when you leave the church or the temple, you are going to be more open-minded and more joyful, because that teaching is going to help you to be more connected with your people and to be filled with more love and understanding. I have faith but I am not the faith. My faith is not the truth yet. We still have ego and so we are one-sided. We are still narrow-minded and are still 'I'. Until one day when there will be no 'I' and we will be in harmony with all sentient beings and then the truth will be clear. Many people think that they understand the teachings, but when you are learning, you may not necessarily get what the teacher intends to teach you. The teacher realises the teaching and he tries to tell you, but if you are not at his level of insight, you don't quite get it, because it is your own interpretation of the teachings. You need to purify the mind, because the real teacher is your own purity.

Where do I find guidance?

If you have an open state of mind, teaching is everywhere, teaching is in the birds singing, teaching is in the sunshine, teaching is in the moonlight, because when you have a clear mind, you realise the reality and your ignorance vanishes. Now we teach and we think, "This is the truth!" There are bursts of enlightenment, when suddenly you know and realise you have always known. Teaching helps you to work on building the enlightened mind, and after you have cultivated this mind you will realise that you have the wisdom within you and so does everyone else.

Guidance for unpleasant conditions

Some people feel bitter, angry at what others have done to them in their life. What can be done to come to terms with this anger? Bitterness is your deep self healing, sending out the feeling that you have been attached to this emotion for too long. Don't blame others, and say they make you bitter and weak. You have held a grudge for too long. They only hurt you once. You are hurting yourself again and again by not letting go. *You* are draining your energy, not the others. Recognise this and let go of the anger and resentment. It's not what they have done to you. It's what you are doing to yourself.

Some people feel guilty about the evil deeds they have committed during their lives. They want to know how to make amends. It's the same whether you feel bitterness, anger or guilt. Don't let the past bother and irritate you now. Let it go. I don't have to remember all the stuff I did wrong. Actions cause consequences, and that is the way things are. Agonising or fuming about them does not change them. Only action in the present will create a different future. Those negative emotions defile the present mind. Arrogance is also a defiled mind. Depression or whatever discomfort I feel is the deep self trying to help me get rid of the past. There are no good actions or bad actions. The defiled mind makes them good or bad. If the mind is not defiled, action is not labelled as good or bad, it's just action. The defiled mind makes it good or bad.

Doing good works

Someone may think, "I am not Mother Theresa. But I would like to do something of value. How can I reshape my life?" You can do that by loving the people close to you. You don't have to be Mother Theresa. Just love the people around you. Those around us will bring our beauty out. Only those who love us can help us learn to protect and not harm or disturb others. We learn that because we have been motivated by them, trained by them to love others wherever we go. And that is Mother Theresa. She was prepared by the people around her to be Mother Theresa. Don't try to build a high-rise building without a foundation. The few people close to you prepare you gently to become friendly and loving wherever you go.

True compassion

Compassion has no extremes, no hate, no love, but is just whatever is needed, whatever is required at that moment. Before I meet you, I don't think, 'Oh, I must help you'. But when I see you, I help you and when I leave you, I don't think about it. Compassion is spontaneous. I'm sure Jesus Christ and the Lord Buddha tried very hard to teach us this, but generally people don't understand it, because we still have conditioned minds now. We want to make love stronger than hate, but if you attach to one thing you attach to the opposite because of the conditioning of our minds. To reach the deepest wisdom, we need to move away from the extremes of love and hate, and let them both go. Then we will find serenity.

Believing in God

"If you believe in God, you are going to be saved," is what we are told. What is God? God is justice, God is fairness, God is kindness, God is no self. You think that if you believe in God, you'll be saved. What is saved? It means you are free from anger, you're free from hatred, you're free from injustice, you're free from torture and suffering and ignorance. All the suffering is from the mind. I'm sure God and Buddha never punished. Punishment is from inside ourselves. For example if I already have a plan in my mind, I won't be very flexible. If I don't have any plan, I will be flexible. If I have a plan, I punish myself because I won't accept anyone else's plan. Now we are loaded with many imprints and perspectives that are blocking this reality. Whereas with an open mind, you flow into the reality and that reality is God. When you flow into the reality, the new mind is fresh, unique and wholesome again.

Don't let the teachings, the names, the labels, the dogma or the doctrines separate us. We should not be separate from Muslims or Christians or the traditional Shamans and healers. We should become more as one, because all the teachings are intended to bring us together. The fact is that there is no need for teaching. If we need teaching now, it's because we are ignorant and need some guidance, but don't study too many teachings and block your clarity. The teaching doesn't need to exist. The heart's openness is the point. If I point my finger to the moon, don't look at my finger, look at the moon. You can learn from the sky, you can learn from animals, you can learn from anything. You learn in order to purify your mind so that you can find the Lord and Buddha within you. And that is religion.

Spirituality

Leaving religion aside, how do we become more spiritual? What is spiritual? It's lighting up the mind. We all have that clear mind. God's mind, one mind, enlightened mind. Because the ego is defiling our clear mind, to become spiritual we need to get rid of defilement. How do we do that? You must be in contact with the physical world to know who you are. Without physical contact you don't see life. Without possessions you don't see your own greed. Without competition, you don't see your own pride. *So we have to be in the world to be free from the world.* You don't become spiritual in isolation on a mountain top, because you are not tempted by the physical practical world there. Away from the everyday world you hide your problems within you. You think you are spiritual but you're just hiding. Involve yourself in day to day life to find your spiritual nature.

Peace and happiness for others

You cannot bring peace and happiness to others. You never will. You can only work for the benefit of others by letting go of your own ego and balancing yourself. If you are balanced at that moment, you can protect your friends from letting out their own demons. You can protect them from more defilement. You can only avoid disturbing them by being balanced. Your balance must be from your own practice. When we are peaceful and in harmony, we can protect others from gathering more defilements, but each one has his own journey.

Finding true values, getting rid of old habits

How can I reconstruct my life to be more ethical and reflect my true values? First, how do you know what your true values are? There is no destruction and no reconstruction. There are no true values and no false values. We have to be with a group of people who help to guide us, and who are our role models before we know what are true and false values. After learning from this support group who leads a balanced life, we can develop values that are right for us. As long as we don't stir up the past again, we don't have to remedy the past. If it's not what you wanted, don't do it again. You need to be protected by your support group from those repeated actions. People think they have to remedy the past. That's not necessary. The present is destined by the past. 'Now' has no freedom. How do you reconstruct your life? You just don't let the old patterns take control. You are easily doomed by the past if you follow the trends of the past. By knowing your past, you can choose the ethical choice. People with a messy past life will find it hard to appreciate the new path in the moment. They are not sensitive enough to realise there is a moment to escape the past and the moment is now. It's like being in a dark room. You don't have to bump into things, and feel them to find out which is a table and which is a chair. You only have to turn on the light. No matter how messy your life was in the past, it doesn't matter. Your life is only here in this moment. Appreciate the moment and you have a wholesome, pure life.

Where can I find people who share my values?

In Buddhism we talk about the Sangha. That is a group of people who are walking the Dharma path, who are following the precepts and living a mindful life. However, if you didn't have a good foundation from the past, and with your first family, it will be very difficult for you to move higher to liberation. Your mind could be closed no matter who you are with, no matter what group you join. I can take you to a sangha[1] or church group, but they cannot reach you, because your mind is closed. On the other hand, if you are already moving towards enlightenment, you will easily find the message, the support that you want for further personal growth. The truth is never separated from the open mind. If your mind is open you will find your sangha anywhere. No *sangha* inside. No *sangha* outside.

Guidelines for living a decent life

Honesty is the best virtue. Let whatever is in your mind be expressed, in the most kindly way you can. Let it go. Speak it out. Clean it out, clear it away. That is best practice. If you are always expressing yourself honestly, and letting the thoughts out honestly, then you will never be angry. Anger is from suppressing your honesty. Arguing with people in a bad temper means that you didn't have proper conversations before. People have a tendency to suppress the feelings within them. But those feelings will bubble up again if they are not acknowledged. When you have those feelings, your deep self is trying to bring healing power, healing nature. You feel discomfort and pressure from your inner self trying to get rid of the dishonesty and the false attachments. Eventually the pressure will force you to express yourself in a harsh way, in anger. Honesty is really letting go. Do it sooner, rather than later.

---

[1] *Support group of one's fellow Buddhist practitioners, more formally from Buddhist monks and/or nuns at your temple.*

Is there such a thing as heaven?

Words are very misleading. Words direct the mind, guiding, helping the mind to make images, and build concepts and notions. We make a drawing of the world through our words. But we don't really understand. As long as we need to have a word to guide us somewhere it means we're not there yet. "Heaven is there." The words are pointing. If we say heaven is somewhere else, we're not there yet. Many people talk about heaven, but everyone is guessing. The notion of 'Heaven' is a way of teaching us to realise that we have a way to go to reach purity. We are defiled as humans and we need to purify ourselves to find heaven. Heaven is a way of teaching us that we should cultivate the state of a heavenly mind. We use different names to express the same state of mind. Heaven is a way of cultivating the mind to purify it. God's mind is not a human mind. We need to purify ourselves to know God's mind. When we know God's mind we will find heaven.

Who am I?

Only you know who you are. You will find out by looking within. If you are ignorant, you see nothing wrong with you. If you are more purified you will see more shortcomings. Lots of practitioners after many years will see more drawbacks in themselves, but people who start to practice see nothing that needs to be changed. They think, "I didn't do anything wrong. I am a good person. Why do I need to practice?" As you practice you become more sensitive to seeing the ego working, affecting your mind. A person who sees people in a positive way, who is happy to be connected with nature and people, is practicing in the right direction. If you need to be separated from people, to get away from people, you have a lot of practice to do. When you are balanced, you are in the world, but you are not going or coming, or controlled by the world. You are here. You will know who you are. You are in the world, but not of it.

Why am I here?

You made the choice to be here, even if you've forgotten, because there's unfinished business for you to deal with. Your unsettled mind has too many attachments to love, to hate. You need to learn how to detach from your cravings, aversions and ignorance. We make a choice to be born, to free ourselves from that unsatisfied need, to make that personal journey to gain wisdom, but after we come we are so burdened with that unfinished business, that we forget we have come here to free ourselves from attachments.

What is attachment? You attach yourself to concepts – if you can look around you in the present moment and appreciate the plants, this room, this cup of tea, this is not attachment. Attachment means that you are attached to the cup of tea you had yesterday, the family gathering from last year. You are attached to concepts and the past. To enjoy and love the contact and experiences at this moment, that is not attachment. To free yourself from attachment, just be here in the moment. Attach to the present! Go from the past! Come here! Wake up! Come into the present! That is what we call detachment, and that is what we are here to learn.

Searching for meaning

People ask, "How do we find meaning in our lives?" The question is really should you be searching for meaning in your life? When you are searching for meaning, that means you are not truly alive. You may exist, but you are not mindful and aware, right here, right now. If you have a need to find meaning, it may sadden you to know that meaning is not to be found. But the truth is that you are not mindful. When you need meaning, the best thing you can do is to let the need go. Realise that you are not here, not alive, not awakened, when you are thinking rather than being.

What is the meaning of life?

Don't even worry about the meaning of life. If you live your life in the moment, if you appreciate this moment, you will have a wholesome life. Never judge if things are good or bad. Move away from judgements. Be detached but compassionate to strangers or family, and you will never be depressed or hurt, never feel tired or want to retire. You are forever and you are connected with all beings. You are so spiritual, so balanced within yourself, so blessed with natural resources, because you appreciate life. You have it all. To live life in the moment - that is liberation from poverty, ignorance, self-denial, arrogance, greed and anger. It would be wonderful if everyone could reach the insight that Pureland is right here.

Where am I on the path?

How do we know how far we have reached towards the goal of enlightenment? After doing homework and studying for some years, we may realise that there's so much more to learn. But sometimes we study, or read and reach a sudden awareness. How far do we still have to go after such an experience?

Anger invites anger. Love invites love. What you realise is always with you. It only has to wait until the condition is right before you are aware of it. So we are all doing the work of awakening every day of our lives. Most of the time, we are not aware. So we have to be shocked by one sentence, by one expression, by one sound or whatever, because we are so accustomed to thinking rather than being. Thought ignores reality. Only a clear mind can realise the truth. The truth is not what you think it is. If it is what you think it is, you will be in it, not out somewhere else being joyful or sad. If we are fully enlightened, we are free of wrong or right, good or bad, understanding or not understanding. This wisdom is innate, in each of us. All we have to do is wake up and know that it is so.

Buddhist basics

Buddhist Basics

Buddhism is not a religion in the true sense of the word, in that it does not deal with our relationship with God. It is better explained as a philosophical guide on how to modify one's own behaviour and thinking in order to reach peace and wisdom. Thich Nhat Hanh, the Vietnamese monk who has written extensively in English about Buddhism, says, "Buddhism is a clever way of enjoying life. Happiness is available. Please help yourself."[1] The Buddhist road to peace and wisdom and greater harmony is not one of suffering and pain, but one of increasing awareness and happiness.

How indeed does one begin to live in greater harmony with others? Gautama Siddartha, the Buddha, spent a large part of his life finding the answer. Siddartha was born a prince in a royal family, and lived a comfortable life, shielded from the realities of sickness, aging and death. When, as a young man, he became aware of these sufferings, and saw a monk who appeared calm and tranquil in the face of such suffering, he decided to leave his comfortable but frivolous life and become a seeker of wisdom. This route took him through many experiences, as the student of different gurus. He found that by following the monastic practices of the day that he failed to find the answers he was looking for. The ascetic life did not give him the truth he sought. Close to starvation, he was offered food by a kindly lay person, and decided that there must be another answer than starvation and self-mortification. He vowed to sit under the Bodhi Tree till he reached enlightenment, and that is what he did. Having confronted mental and spiritual experiences of the most bizarre and horrifying kinds, and understood them, he found himself awake to the truths of existence. 'Budh' means 'to wake up'. The Buddha is one who is completely awake. He wanted to share his understanding with others, and started teaching the path that he found that allowed him to wake up.

The Four Noble Truths

What was that path? The Buddha identified four Noble Truths.

❑ There is suffering

❑ There are the causes of suffering

---

[1] As quoted by Christina Feldman in "The Buddhist Path to Simplicity"

❑ There is a way to escape from suffering

❑ The escape is to follow the Noble Eightfold Path.

Put simply, suffering comes from our cravings, aversions and ignorance, and our attachments to the past. In experiencing cravings, we lust after things, we desire them. These could be people, possessions, status, pleasures, beliefs and ideas. This attachment to things causes us pain, because we cling to things that must pass, or have already gone. Life is always changing. We need to learn how to let go. Our aversions - feelings of revulsion, hatred and dislike - also cause us suffering. The ties that bind us to our enemies are often stronger than those that bind us to our loved ones. This also causes us great suffering. Ignorance - not understanding the truth about things - also causes great suffering. We are misinformed and misguided and we do not understand the causes and conditions that create the world around us and how we experience it. We also cause our own suffering, by our own actions.

> **By oneself the evil is done, and it is oneself who suffers:**
>
> **by oneself the evil is not done, and by one's Self one becomes pure.**
>
> **The pure and the impure come from oneself:**
>
> **no man can purify another."**
>
> **Dhammapada 165**

This is the simple description of Karma. Karma is often misunderstood to be a punishment of some kind. Not at all. It is just a universal force that contains no blame and no recriminations. It is the way it is. The acts we choose to do have consequences. How does one deal with karma? We learn to lead a simple life, causing harm to none. Even though we may be suffering as a result of previous actions, we concentrate on how we act in the present, knowing that as we change our behaviour, and gradually learn to act more mindfully and with greater caring, and do less harm, so the unpleasant circumstances will fade. There is no sense that we are 'fated' to suffer greatly. Having deliberately committed a harmful crime, our response to it, our feelings of remorse, our desire to be different, our kindly acts to the victims of our act, all help us to re-write our future. It is only knowing, deliberate acts that affect one's karma. Accidental hurt caused to others is not considered a karmic act. There needs to be both the intention to do harm, and the act itself in order for there to be a karmic liability. But even if our past actions have been lacking in skill and wisdom, there is no need to suffer endlessly. The Buddha has drawn a path for people to follow if they wish to end their suffering.

The Eightfold Path

This path is simple to describe but not as easy to follow, because it requires effort. In fact, right effort is one of the eight requirements. The Eightfold path contains guides to behaviour. Applying these guides to our behaviour, we find that our lives become less complicated, less painful and less full of suffering. The Buddha said, "Sughadda, it is not important whether you are fully enlightened. The question is whether you want to liberate yourself. If you do, practice the Noble Eightfold Path. Wherever the Noble Eightfold Path is practiced, joy, peace and insight are there."[2] The Buddha taught this path in his first Dharma talk, and continued to teach it for 45 years, till his death.

There are eight elements to work on, when following this path. They are:

Right view, right thinking, right speech, right action, right livelihood, right diligence, right mindfulness and right concentration. How do we know what is right? Here are some pointers:

Right View[3]

Right view needs a deep understanding of the wisdom of the Four Noble Truths, and the faith and confidence that there are people who have been able to transform their suffering.

Right Thinking

The Buddha said:

"The thought manifests as the word;

The word manifests as the deed;

The deed develops into habit;

And habit hardens into character.

So watch the thought and its ways with care,

And let it spring from love

Born out of concern for all beings."

---

[2] *Mahaparinibbana Sutta, Digha Nikaya 16*

[3] *The discussion on the eightfold path is based on Thich Nhat Hanh's explanations in his book, "The Heart of the Buddha's Teaching"*

Thinking is the speech of our mind, and thinking leads to action. When we have the right view, it is easier to develop right thinking. Right thinking is hard to practice when one's mind wanders and jumps around. But there are ways to pull one's mind back into the present moment. You can ask yourself **"Am I sure?"** Are things the way you think they are? Are you making assumptions without checking them out? Jumping to wrong conclusions is not right thinking. Wasting time and energy thinking about the past without being aware of the present increase pain and suffering. Ask yourself **"What am I doing?"** to return yourself to the present moment. **"Hello, habit!"** is another practice that helps us in right thinking. We have habits that have built up over the years that are not useful to us, and cause us to suffer. We can watch these habitual ways of thinking, and when we notice them, we can change them. Finally, check with yourself, **"Is this a kind thought?"** Our deep wish to help others and stop causing harm helps guide our thinking along the right paths.

Right Speech

Right thinking helps to bring about right speech. Right speech is honest and kindly, and does not exaggerate or embellish the truth. Learning to stop and think before we talk is a good step to developing right speech. This is being mindful of our spoken and written words. Hurtful and dishonest words do great damage and can cause us and the people around us great suffering.

Right Action

How do you know if your actions are right? They are right if they are kindly and do no harm. Non-violence to ourselves and others is right action. Our actions are also guided by mindfulness, so we are more likely to do right action if we are aware all the time of what is going on, and we act in full awareness of the intended and unintended consequences of our course of action.

Right livelihood

Earning a living takes most of our time. If we are engaged in work that harms ourselves or others, or that hurts people or animals or plants or the environment, how can that be the right way to make a living? Examine what you do every day to earn money, and if you are causing harm in your work, see how you can change it. It is better to do work that helps others, even if you lose income or status. You cannot be peaceful or happy if you are engaged in destructive activities much of the time.

Right effort, or right diligence

In order to grow in wisdom, we need to put in some effort. It's like studying to pass exams. You have to make the effort to improve. Right effort is taking the trouble to apply the principles, regularly and with energy and commitment. Right diligence will bring us the reward of increasing peace and happiness. If we are working hard to collect material possessions, or indulge in meaningless pleasures, this will not bring us peace, because it would not be right effort. This is not to say that we must punish ourselves and force ourselves to do hours of meditation, to contort our body into funny positions, or starve ourselves. The Buddha asked the monk Sona, "Is it true that before you became a monk you were a musician?" Sona replied that it was so. The Buddha asked, "What happens if the string of your instrument is too loose?"

"When you pluck it, there will be no sound," Sona replied.

"What happens when the string is too taut?"

"It will break."

"The practice of the Way is the same," the Buddha said. "Maintain your health. Be joyful. Do not force yourself to do things you cannot do."[4]

So we do what we can, gently working towards a better understanding of life, walking the middle path.

Right Mindfulness

Mindfulness is the key to Buddhist practice. Even though each part of the eightfold path supports the others, mindfulness is at the heart of the Buddha's teachings. Mindfulness is remembering to come back to the present moment. Being mindful is being attentive and heedful, giving our full attention to what we are doing. Being present in the moment is being mindful. Staying mindfully in the present is probably the most important work you can do in finding peace and happiness. There are ways to help us stay fully in the present. One is to give our full attention to what we are doing. The Zen koan says, "When walking, just walk. When sitting, just sit." Another is to attempt to touch deeply what we see around us, the person, the work, the tree. Another is to listen deeply, so we can truly begin to understand. By deep listening, we can help relieve other people's suffering. Sometimes just the knowledge that you are there and that you care is enough. When we are mindful, we often realise,

---

[4] *Vinaya Mahavagga Khuddaka Nikaya 5*

"Oh, of course, I see, I understand!" It is mindfulness and full attention that allows us to reach understanding.

Right Concentration

Mindfulness brings concentration. Concentration means focus. We leave everything else and focus fully on something. We use concentration to give our full attention to what we are doing. Concentration gives us stability and stillness. When you are deeply concentrated, you are absorbed in the moment. You become the moment. The most creative people have this ability to focus and concentrate fully on their work, and it is this deep concentration that allows humans to express their greatest talents. Concentration is an important aspect of Buddhist meditation. Through concentration we also learn to confront our suffering. We don't run away from it. Sometimes we need to escape our problems for relief, but at some stage we have to return to face them.

Meditation

Meditation is part of many eastern religious practices, and has become more and more popular in the West, for good reason. In Buddhism, our attention is directed to remain in the present, focusing deeply on the object of our meditation. Meditation enhances the quality of our concentration. In some religious practices, meditation can be used to escape from suffering, rather than to realise the liberation that comes with insight into our suffering. Insight meditation is the practice of focusing on how our mind works and how we react. This focus helps to bring insight. We also meditate to cultivate the skilful qualities of our mind, particularly mindfulness. Cultivating mindfulness through meditation is like building physical stamina. You do it regularly and find that gradually over time you become more fit and more accomplished.

Insight meditation is not run by a fixed set of rules. Individual practice is based on your own self-enquiry into what works for you. Finding a teacher and a safe, calm place to meditate are very important in meditation practice. Often, two major meditation practices are taught at a beginner level. The first is meditation on the breath, where you concentrate on your breathing, in and out. There are various ways of doing this, which a beginner's meditation class will explain clearly. The second kind of meditation is on loving kindness or compassion, where one concentrates on sending love and kindness to oneself, then to one's loved ones and gradually to all beings in the universe. Both practices bring peace and calm and a sense of being at one with the world. Meditation can be done sitting, standing, walking or lying down. Walking meditation incorporates movement into the concentration, so the movements of the body also become elements to concentrate on.

There are many books written about meditation. It is worthwhile reading more, and getting guidance in this incredibly valuable practice. One thing to bear in mind is that the practice of Buddhism is not limited to the minutes or hours one spends in meditation. The real practice of Buddhism is ongoing and takes place in every hour, minute and second of life that is lived mindfully, in the present moment. Meditation is a part of a mindful life, but not the whole of it.

The five precepts

The five precepts or mindfulness practices are guidelines to follow in our behaviour. They are moral codes. These are not laws that cannot be broken, as in the Ten Commandments of Christianity. They are principles describing behaviour that will bring us greater happiness. They can be followed by Buddhists and non-Buddhists alike. We practice the precepts because we know that this kind of behaviour guards us from doing harm, and shows kindness to others. Sometimes we fail. But we keep on trying.

Good Buddhists remind themselves to follow the five precepts daily. They are to:

- ❑ Refrain from killing living creatures
- ❑ Refrain from taking what is not freely given
- ❑ Refrain from sexual misconduct
- ❑ Refrain from false speech
- ❑ Refrain from taking in harmful substances, such as intoxicating drugs and liquor.

The Five Ennoblers

While the five precepts tell us what to avoid, the Five Ennoblers tell us which qualities to cultivate. They are:

- ❑ Loving kindness
- ❑ Renunciation
- ❑ Contentment
- ❑ Truthfulness
- ❑ Mindfulness.

So we are not only guided in what to stay away from, but also what to work towards.

The five precepts are those practiced by lay people. On special religious days, Buddhists may choose to practice further precepts. Buddhist monks and nuns practice far more precepts, as a way of enriching and stabilizing their deep search for spiritual enlightenment.

Where to from here?

There are more and more Buddhist centres springing up in the Western World. Use the Internet to find the closest centre to you.

Useful books about Buddhism

Dalai Lama, His Holiness, the. (2002). *How to Practise – the Way to a Meaningful Life.* London: Rider Books. A short, simply written Tibetan Buddhist guide to Buddhist techniques for gaining mental peace and compassion.

Das, Lama Surya. (1999). *Awakening to the Sacred.* London: Bantam Books. A relaxed and easy western introduction to the spirit and spiritual practice.

Dhammananda, Dr K. Sri. (2000). *What Buddhists Believe.* Malaysia: Buddhist Missionary Society. A sensible, easy-to-read explanation of Buddhism history, philosophy and practice.

Feldman, Christina. (2001). *The Buddhist Path to Simplicity – Spiritual Practice for Everyday Life.* London: Thorsons. A gentle introduction to the simple life, from a western point of view.

Hanh, Thich Nhat. (2001). *Anger – Buddhist wisdom for cooling the flames.* London: Random House. Written after the 9/11 bombings in New York, this book gives simple, kindly advice on dealing with anger.

Hanh, Thich Nhat. (1999). *Going Home – Jesus and Buddha as brothers.* New York: Riverhead Books. Explores the links and similarities between Buddhism and Christianity in a gentle, sensitive way.

Hanh, Thich Nhat. (1998). *The Heart of the Buddha's Teaching – Transforming Suffering into Peace, Joy and Liberation.* New York: Broadway Books. A remarkable English explanation of the major elements of Buddhist philosophy; a marvellous, easy-to-read reference work.

Shen, C T. *Mayflower II.* Malaysia: Copyright Holder: The Institute for Advanced Studies of World Religions. Donated by: The Corporate Body of the Buddha Educational Foundation. This book is quite scientific in its approach and is made up of a collection of speeches delivered in the USA by Mr C T Shen.

It covers all the Buddhist concepts in a clear but analytical style.

Sumedho, Ajahn. (1991). *The Way It Is.* Malaysia: Amaravati Publications. Donated for free distribution by The Corporate Body of the Buddha Educational Foundation. This book contains a collection of teachings by Ajahn Sumedho in the Theravadin tradition for people who have some experience of meditation. Ajahn Sumedho is an ordained

Theravadin Bikkhu (1966). He is American by birth and studied under the very revered Ven. Ajahn Chah. His style of writing is humorous and succinct - very down to earth. Great to return to again and again. Each essay is relatively short, so it is not a huge challenge to read this book.

Sumedho, Ajahn. (1987). **Mindfulness: The Path to the Deathless.** Publications For free distribution. This is a small book on his meditation techniques, again very practical and down-to-earth. Designed to help people learning to meditate.

Weisman, Arinna and Smith, Jean. (2001). **The Beginner's Guide to Insight Meditation.** New York: Bell Tower. A simple, thoughtful Western guide to beginning meditation practice.